IRONBARK PRESS

Fatty's BIG BBQ BOOK

Compiled by
GAIL STANTON

with
PAUL VAUTIN

Food styling
Penny Farrell

Food Photography
Rowan Fotheringham

Location Photography
Ern MacQuillan

IRONBARK
PRESS

Published in 1993 by Ironbark Press
Level 1, 175 Alison Road, Randwick NSW 2031

© Gail Stanton and Paul Vautin

National Library Of Australia
Cataloguing-in-Publication

> Stanton, Gail. Fatty's Big BBQ Book.
> Includes index.
>
> ISBN 1 875471 27 8
>
> 1. BBQ cookery.
> I. Title. II. Title: Fatty's Big BBQ Book.

641.5784

ABOUT THE AUTHORS:

GAIL STANTON

Food in all its myriad guises has been the consuming interest of Gail Stanton for much of her working life. For the past 10 years she has been a partner and creative force in *Cuisine Affaire* — the Sydney-based company which caters with style and flair for corporate and private gatherings from 12 to 1200. As well as any food expert in the land Gail has tapped into the the changing way of things in Australia as the growing multi-culturalism has altered our approach to food and eating. She is an innovator in the areas of new flavours and fresh ideas in food — and it's an approach that surfaces in many exciting ways in the hundreds of recipes in this book. Gail's partnership with Fatty Vautin in *Fatty's Big BBQ Book* threatens to transform the traditional steaks-'n-snags Aussie BBQ into a varied and exciting culinary experience. Gail is also a super-keen footy fan, and reckons there's nothing better than some al fresco dining — before or after the game.

PAUL "FATTY" VAUTIN

Those who know Fatty Vautin will declare with confidence that his performances with the knife and fork (or hovering beside the BBQ) match anything he ever achieved on the football field. If that's the case Fatty could be judged a trencherman of exceptional quantity. A brilliant rugby league career which ended in 1991, gained him almost every laurel in the game. Signed by Ken Arthurson from Brisbane Wests in 1979, Vautin began an outstanding career in Sydney premiership football — 11 seasons and 204 first grade games with Manly and two seasons and 34 games with Easts. He captained Manly to win the 1987 premiership, played 21 games with crack English club St Helens in season 1988-89 including the Wembley Cup final, played 22 State of Origin games between 1982-90 — and 13 Test matches. A robust, never-say-die second rower or lock Vautin became one of the great crowd-pleasers of modern football. On his retirement from the game at the end of 1991 his career in the media blossomed. Regular Friday appearances on Ray Martin's *Midday Show* turned him into a national celebrity. He became an ace football commentator with Channel 9, and compere of the high-rating *Footy Show*. Through his appearances in the immensely successful Toohey's *World's Biggest BBQ* ads in 1993 he became the best known redhead in Australia. He was munching a sausage in a roll when approached with the idea of Fatty's *Big BBQ Book*. "I won't even have to get back to you on that!" he replied ...

THANKS

Ironbark Press wishes to thank the many people and organisations who contributed to this book in many different ways. They are listed below in no particular order:

Tooheys for giving us the opportunity to join in the fun, and in particular Adam Oakes and Sharon Pelham at the World's Biggest BBQ headquarters

Margaret McDonagh and her colleagues at Barbeques Galore

Buttercup Bakeries

Rosella (for the sauce!)

Jo and Sam at Antico's Fruit Market, Northbridge Plaza

Annie Ford and the Fish Marketing Authority's Sydney Seafood School

Enoteca Sileno at Pyrmont for the wonderful cheeses used in recipes thoughout this book

Bush Tucker Supply Company for the produce used in developing the Bush Tucker section in this book

Contents

UNDER COVER ... 9
JUST KEBABS ... 13
PICNIC IN THE PARK ... 21
VEGGIES AND SALADS ... 27
A BIT ON THE SIDE ... 33
GOURMET BARBIE ... 37
SOMETHING SAUCY ... 41
AFTER THE GAME ... 47
TABLE FOR TWO ... 51
RISE AND SHINE ... 55
SNAGS GALORE ... 59
BIG 'N BEEFY ... 62
GONE FISHIN' ... 77
FEATHERED FRIENDS ... 87
BUSH TUCKER ... 93
FATTY'S FAVOURITES ... 99
BACHELORS' BASICS ... 103
ONLY OYSTERS ... 109
MOTHERS' DAY ... 111
PERFECT ENDING ... 117

Foreword

It seems perfectly logical that the career of a footballer known universally as "Fatty" would one day veer in the direction of food. Paul "Fatty" Vautin in fact was never really that — a fatty — although he admits to being a mite chubby when he came from Brisbane to Sydney in 1979, seeking fame and fortune on the rugby league playing fields. Fatty Vautin found a fair measure of both, especially sporting fame, as he built a career which took him all the way to the top — an Australian Test jumper, an impeccable State of Origin record, and the supreme honour of captaining a winning premiership side (Manly, 1987). Fatty played his football at a rock hard 95 kilograms and two years after he clocked up his last game (for Easts in August 1991) was still nudging the scales at 95 kilos as he confronted, with some amazement, a rapidly expanding and enormously successful business career. Despite his comparitive svelteness, Fatty, however, freely admits to loving his tucker ... and *especially* a good old Aussie BBQ.

His selection by Tooheys in 1993 to be the focal point of the company's sensational *World's Biggest BBQ* promotion turned out to be one of the advertising masterstrokes of modern times. The buildup to the October '93 BBQ('s) through a series of television ads as an increasingly worried Fatty confronted the problems of staging a gigantic barbie, captivated public interest — and became the most talked-about campaign in years.

Somehow Fatty Vautin and an Aussie BBQ seemed a perfect match. The red-haired knockabout who became a national TV identity, via Ray Martin's *Midday Show*, then a TV football commentator and host, declares with enthusiasm that there is absolutely nothing better in life than a barbie with friends on a balmy summer's day. The Vautin formula for the perfect BBQ contains the following essential ingredients: sausages, mushrooms, onions, tomato sauce, mates, form guide, transistor.

Such a blend on a sparkling December day, he reckons, is about as close to heaven on earth as you can get.

Fatty's love affair with food, however, is nowhere near as basic as his tongue in cheek "perfect barbie" formula would suggest. Vautin, in fact, is something of a connoisseur of food in (almost) all its wonderful guises, an interest honed by the world travelling he has done via his football. He has wide and contrasting tastes in eating, drawing the line, however, at Kangaroo steaks. "Can you imagine a rump of (Artie) Beetson or sirloin of (Paul) Sironen with onions?" he asks. "The prospect is too awful to contemplate and you can leave me right out. In fact I won't even get back to you on that"...

In *Fatty's Big BBQ Book*, Vautin brought his great interest in food to a supremely logical conclusion, via a brilliant partnership with one of the country's leading gourmet cooks,

Sydney-based Gail Stanton. Gail's recipes for the book, ranging all the way from the super-simple to the spectacular represent the state of the art in BBQ cooking. Gail's background for such a book, working alongside a footballer for whom "claret" represented what came out when you copped one on the field and "steak" the thing you put on a black eye — was impeccable.

For the last 10 years Gail has been a principal in the Sydney-based corporate catering company *Cuisine Affaire*, whose reputation for excellence is unsurpassed in the field. Gail calls her love affair with food "a hobby that got out of hand". Gail has been at the cutting edge of the rapid changes in changing tastes and more adventurous approach to food that has characterised Australian society in the last decade. As you will come to realise in the mouth-watering pages ahead even the humble barbie has taken a quantum leap from the old burnt snags and steaks days when it's in the hands of someone like Gail Stanton. Gail's partnership with Fatty Vautin in this book was a symbiotic one. Married to Frank Stanton, the former ground-breaking national coach who masterminded the deeds of the 1982 Kangaroo *Invincibles*, Gail is a keen rugby league fan, and rarely misses a Manly game. Gail's interest in league and Fatty's in food made it a perfect match.

Fatty's Big BBQ Book is something completely different. Featuring the superb food photography of Rowan Fotheringham and location photography of Ern McQuillan and the consistently creative input of Gail Stanton it is a wonderful guide to the art of BBQ cooking ... and of doing it in style. But it is also irreverently Fatty's too. His special recipes take pride of place — and his often hilarious observations on food, BBQ's and life are dotted through its pages.

The book follows in the footsteps of the hugely successful Vautin biography *Fatty — the strife and times of Paul Vautin* (by Mike Colman), and confirms the former champ of the football field as one of the great characters of modern Australian life. Fatty remains unspoiled by all the success, and is still in many ways the knockabout from next door who just happened to play a bit of footy.

He's just the sort of bloke who would bung on a barbie, and invite a few friends. As a matter of fact, now that we've mentioned it ...

— **Ian Heads**

UNDER *Cover*

* The recipes in this section are particularly suited to covered barbeque cooking. For other covered cooking recipes see page 121.

BEEF SPARE RIBS

1kg beef spare ribs
1/2 cup spicy tomato sauce
good dash worcestershire sauce
2 teaspoons kecap manis
2 tablespoons water
2 tablespoons grapeseed oil
1 teaspoon sambal oelek
1 teaspoon honey

Combine all marinade ingredients until well mixed. Allow ribs to marinate for at least 4 hours. Cook on the barbeque with the lid on for 20-25 minutes over indirect heat. Baste with the marinade from time to time during cooking.

MARINATED CHICKEN LEGS

8 chicken legs
1/2 cup orange juice
1/2 cup pineapple juice
1/2 teaspoon dry mustard
1 teaspoon curry powder
1 tablespoon sweet chilli sauce
1 tablespoon soy sauce

Combine orange juice, pineapple juice, mustard, curry powder, sweet chilli sauce and soy sauce. Cover chicken legs with this sauce and leave to marinate for several hours. Remove from marinade and barbeque until tender, turning frequently and brushing with marinade. Reduce remaining marinade and use to sauce chicken. This recipe works well in a covered barbeque or using a hooded barbeque with indirect heat.

BABY GOLDEN NUGGET PUMPKIN

These tasty little pumpkins need only to be put on the barbeque over indirect heat with the lid on, for about an hour. They can be cooked in a similar way in the covered barbeque. When cooked, core out the centre piece containing the seeds and fill with sour cream and chives or **Bacon and Sour Cream Sauce** (page 42). Serve one per person.

BEER CAKE

60 g butter, room temperature
2 cups self-raising flour
1 cup Tooheys Draught beer
1 egg, well beaten
1/2 cup sugar
1 cup walnuts, chopped
1/2 teaspoon cinnamon
grated rind 1/2 orange
2 tablespoons butter
sugar
coconut

Combine butter and flour. Add beer, egg, sugar, nuts, cinnamon and orange rind, beating until a batter-like consistency. Meanwhile, butter a 18cm cake tin or similar size foil tray. Spoon cake mixture into tin and cook over a low fire with lid on, for about 30 minutes. When cake is cooked and still warm, spread with butter and sprinkle with sugar and coconut. Serve at once (with lashings of cream if you wish).

GLAZED PORK NECK

1 kg piece pork neck or loin of pork
1/2 cup white wine
1/4 cup orange juice
1/4 cup vegetable or grapeseed oil
1/4 cup apricot conserve
1 small red chilli, finely chopped
3 cloves garlic, finely chopped
1 teaspoon ginger
1 teaspoon oregano
ground black pepper

If using loin of pork, remove rind and trim away excess fat. Meanwhile, in a saucepan combine wine, orange juice, oil, apricot conserve, chilli, garlic, ginger, oregano and pepper. Reduce mixture to half and brush over pork, covering well. Cook pork in covered barbeque over a medium heat, with lid on, for approximately 3/4 — 1 hour. Continue to baste during cooking. Pork rind can be oiled and salted and cooked alongside pork. The marinade can be reduced and served as a sauce.

BEER DAMPER

3 cups self-raising flour
1 level teaspoon salt
3/4 cup milk
3/4 cup Tooheys Draught beer

Sift the flour and salt together and add enough of the liquid to form a thick, sticky dough. Dust hands with flour and form into a round loaf. Dust lightly with flour. Cook in covered barbeque over indirect heat. The baking time will depend on the heat of your fire. It should take around 3/4 hour. The damper can of course be cooked in the kitchen oven.

BREAD AND BUTTER PUDDING

1 continental fruit loaf
butter
3 eggs
3 egg yolks
300mls cream
300mls milk
1 teaspoon vanilla
1/2 teaspoon ground nutmeg
2 tablespoons brown sugar

Slice the fruit loaf and lightly butter each slice. Place slices in a baking dish, cutting to fit. Beat eggs, milk, vanilla, nutmeg and brown sugar. Add cream and beat to combine. Pour over the bread and cook over the indirect heat of a low fire for 30-40 minutes until golden brown.

Fatty's Food For Thought:

REQUIREMENTS FOR AFTER-GAME BARBIE
1. Fence to lean on
2. Steak to put on black eye
3. Well-grassed lawn to cushion fall in case crook knee gives out.
4. Dart board featuring face of match referee.
5. Megaphone to ensure that all at gathering are in no doubt that "we wuz robbed" (to be used only in case of a loss)
6. Humble and modest manner (after a win): "well, they're a very good side and I was just lucky to get those four tries ... the rest of the boys made it easy for me etc etc etc."
7. Unlimited crates of Tooheys.

JUST *Kebabs*

APRICOT LAMB KEBABS

1kg trimmed lamb topside
1 cup apricot nectar
16 dried apricots, sliced in half
2 tablespoons grapeseed oil
1 teaspoon golden syrup
2 cloves garlic, sliced
3-4 sprigs rosemary
freshly ground pepper
1 onion, quartered
red capsicum, cut into chunks

Combine the apricot nectar, dried apricots, oil, golden syrup, garlic, rosemary and pepper. Cut the lamb into cubes and marinate in the mixture for at least 4 hours. Thread onto wooden skewers alternately with the apricot halves, onion and capsicum and cook over hot coals or on the barbeque hotplate, brushing with the marinade. Reduce the marinade to a sauce consistency and serve on kebabs.

BEEF MINCE KEBABS

500g minced beef
1 tablespoon grated onion
1/2 cup breadcrumbs
1 egg beaten
1 tablespoon olive oil
2 teaspoons wine vinegar
1 tablespoon chopped parsley
1 tablespoon chopped mint
1 clove garlic, crushed
2 tablespoons spicy tomato sauce

Combine all ingredients and mix together thoroughly. Leave to stand for several hours or preferably overnight. Form into sausage shapes and secure on the end of long wooden skewers. Refrigerate again for at least an hour. Cook on oiled barbeque hotplate over a moderate heat, turning carefully until cooked on all sides — take care not to overcook as meat will dry out. Makes approximately 12 kebabs. Curry Yoghurt Sauce (page 44) compliments this dish.

Assorted kebabs (pp 14, 16, 17, 18, 20, 38) and *Garlic mushrooms* (p106)

ORIENTAL PRAWN KEBABS

20 green king prawns
1 tablespoon sesame oil
1 tablespoon vegetable oil
3 tablespoons sake
3 tablespoons rice wine vinegar
1/4 cup kecap manis
4 tablespoons brown sugar
2 cloves garlic, crushed
1 tablespoon fresh ginger, finely chopped

Mix together the marinade ingredients. Peel and de-vein prawns, leaving on the tails. Place prawns in marinade and leave for 3-4 hours. Thread 2 or 3 prawns on a wooden skewer and barbeque for a few minutes, until cooked.

TANGY OYSTER KEBABS

1 bottle oysters
bacon rashers
tabasco

Trim rind from bacon rashers, slice bacon in half lengthways and each half into quarters. Drain oysters. Sprinkle bacon with a little (or a lot!) of tabasco sauce and roll each piece. Alternately thread pieces of bacon with 4 oysters onto long wooden skewers. Cook on the barbeque for a few minutes and serve immediately.

GREEK CHEESE KEBABS

250g halloumi cheese
fresh oregano leaves
lemon wedges
freshly ground black pepper

Cut the cheese into cubes. Thread 3 cubes of cheese onto wooden skewers interleaved with fresh oregano leaves. To barbeque, place the skewered cheese on the barbeque hotplate and turn frequently until done. Serve with lemon wedges and freshly ground black pepper. Makes approximately 6 skewers.

BARBEQUED PORK KEBABS

500g pork mince
2 tablespoons soy sauce
1 small onion, chopped
1/2 teaspoon ground ginger
1/2 teaspoon garam masala
1 teaspoon hoi sin sauce
1 teaspoon brown sugar
1 egg, beaten
1/4 cup breadcrumbs

Combine soy sauce, onion, ground ginger, garam masala, hoi sin, brown sugar and beaten egg. Mix well. Add this to the pork mince with the bread crumbs. When all ingredients are thoroughly combined form into sausage shapes. Secure on the end of wooden skewers and refrigerate for 1-2 hours. Cook on oiled barbeque hotplate over moderate heat, turning carefully until cooked on all sides. Take care not to overcook as meat will dry out. Makes approximately 12 kebabs. Try this dish with Mint and Coriander Sauce (page 45).

MARINATED FISH KEBABS

1 kilogram fish fillets
1/2 cup oil
1/4 cup fresh orange juice
1 clove garlic, crushed
1 flat teaspoon sugar
1 teaspoon paprika
3-4 shallots, finely chopped
1 teaspoon grated fresh ginger
1 heaped tablespoon fresh coriander, chopped

Cut fish into large cubes. Combine oil, orange juice, garlic, sugar, paprika, shallots, ginger and coriander. Cover fish with this marinade and return to the fridge for at least 4 hours. Soak wooden skewers in water overnight. Thread several pieces of fish on end of skewers and barbeque until fish is just cooked, brushing with remaining marinade. Serve with Mint and Coriander Sauce (Page 45).

CURRIED CHICKEN KEBABS

500g chicken thigh fillets
2/3 cup coconut milk
2 tablespoons water
1 heaped teaspoon good curry powder
1 flat teaspoon paprika
1 teaspoon brown sugar
1 tablespoon vegetable oil

Combine the coconut milk, water, curry powder, paprika, sugar and oil. Stir until well mixed. Trim thigh fillets of fat and cut into chunks. Place in the mixture and allow to marinate for 2-4 hours. Thread on long wooden skewers and cook on the barbeque hotplate for 5-10 minutes. Serve with Curry Yoghurt Sauce (page 44). Makes 10-12 skewers.

BARBEQUED STRACCHINO

250g stracchino
fresh basil leaves

Cut cheese into cubes of about 2cm. Thread 3 cubes of cheese onto wooden skewers inter-leaved with fresh basil leaves. Fold the basil leaves to a similar size as the cheese. Place in the freezer for at least 2 hours. To barbeque, place the skewered cheese on the barbeque hotplate and turn frequently until cheese begins to melt. Serve immediately. Makes approximately 6 kebabs.

PORK AND PLUM KEBABS

500g pork scotch fillets
1 cup dark grape juice
2 tablespoons plum jam
1 teaspoon hoi sin sauce
1/2 small onion, chopped
1 tablespoon grapeseed oil

Combine the grape juice, plum jam, hoi sin sauce, onion and oil until well mixed. Cut the pork into cubes, place in the mixture and allow to marinate for 2-4 hours. Thread onto long wooden skewers and cook on the barbeque hotplate for 5-10 minutes. Reduce marinade to sauce consistency and serve over kebabs. Makes 10-12 kebabs.

Standing rib roast (p50)

AVOCADO AND PAW PAW STICKS

1 ripe but firm avocado
1 Fijian paw paw
1 tablespoon brown sugar
juice of 1/2 a lemon

Mix together brown sugar and lemon juice. Stir untill sugar has become liquid. Meanwhile, peel and de-seed the avocado and paw paw. Cut into chunks and thread alternately onto long wooden skewers. Brush with sugar and lemon juice mixture and grill on barbeque hotplate for a few minutes. Serve immediately. This is a lovely accompaniment to white meat dishes and most seafoods.

SCALLOP KEBABS

12 scallops
4 thin slices prosciutto
fresh coriander, chopped
lime

Clean scallops and spinkle with lime juice. Fold prosciutto strips lengthwise in half and cut into three, sprinkle with coriander and wrap around scallops, securing with a toothpick. Grill over hot coals or on hot plate of barbeque for a few minutes until scallops are just cooked. (Do not overcook scallops). Finely grated ginger may be substituted for coriander.

Fatty's Food For Thought:
BEFORE THE GAME
I used to rip into a couple of tins of baked beans about ten o'clock on Sunday mornings and by kick-off time at three, I was literally exploding onto the footy field. These days, pasta seems to be more the go.

Picnic IN THE PARK

SPICY CRUSTED LEG OF LAMB

1 medium size leg of lamb

Curry paste:
1/4 cup vegetable oil
2 tablespoons ground coriander
1 tablespoon ground cumin
1 tablespoon ground paprika
2 teaspoons ginger
2 teaspoons turmeric
2 teaspoons mustard seeds
1 teaspoon chilli powder
2 medium onions, finely chopped
2-3 cloves garlic, crushed
50 mls white vinegar
salt and freshly ground pepper

To make paste:
In a saucepan, heat oil until hot. Add all ingredients except vinegar. Cook for 1-2 minutes, stirring occasionally. Add vinegar and cook for a further 1/2 minute. Stores well in fridge.

To crust lamb:
Make sure all the fat has been trimmed from the outside of the lamb (including parchment-like white skin). Coat lamb with paste at least 4 hours before cooking. When barbeque is ready, place lamb in double foil (with shiny side to the inside) and envelope securely. The cooking time will depend on heat and type of barbeque. A medium leg of lamb should take about 1-1 1/2 hours. If you can, plan to allow up to an hour for the lamb to stand before carving (still wrapped in foil and left in a warm spot beside the barbeque) and you will have a wonderfully juicy leg of lamb to carve. When ready to serve, collect juices from inside foil and serve over the sliced lamb.

TOMATO AND BOCCONCINI SALAD

3-4 firm vine-ripened tomatoes
3-4 bocconcini
fresh basil
extra virgin olive oil
freshly ground black pepper

Slice tomatoes and bocconcini and interleave one with the other on a platter. Tear basil finely and spread over tomatoes and cheese. Lightly cover with the olive oil and pepper.

Barbequed marshmallow (p25)

HERBED FLOWER POT BREAD

400g plain flour
1/2 teaspoon salt
25g fresh yeast
1/4 teaspoon sugar
150mls milk, lukewarm
2 eggs, beaten
2 tablespoons butter
1 teaspoon celery seeds
selection of freshly chopped herbs eg. chives, continental parsley, oregano
black sesame seeds (to sprinkle on top)

Sift the flour and salt into a bowl and make a well in the centre. Sprinkle the sugar on the yeast, and cream the yeast while slowly adding the milk. Pour into the well of flour, covering the yeast mixture with a little of the flour. Cover and stand in a warm place for about 20 minutes until yeast begins to work. Combine the eggs with the melted butter, add the herbs and celery seeds. Add this to the flour and yeast mixture and knead until you have a smooth elastic dough. Cover and stand in a warm place until the dough has doubled in size (about 30 minutes). Meanwhile, butter an earthenware flower pot. To prevent the pots cracking and the loaves sticking, grease the pot well the first time you use it, having previously baked it empty in a hot oven for 30 minutes. Knead the dough gently once more and drop it into the flower pot. Leave to stand in a warm place for a further 20 minutes. Brush the top of the loaf with water, sprinkle with black sesame seeds and bake at 180 — 200 C for approximately 30 minutes.

CREAMY POTATO SALAD

1kg baby new potatoes
1 carton sour cream
1/2 bunch shallots, finely sliced
1 tablespoon mustard seeds
salt and freshly cracked black pepper

Gently boil unpeeled new potatoes, taking care not to let them split. Drain. Meanwhile, combine shallots, mustard seeds and salt with the sour cream and mix through the potatoes. Sprinkle with freshly ground black pepper.

CHICKEN SATAYS

4 chicken breast fillets
2 teaspoons light soy
1 tablespoon dark soy
2 tablespoons peanut butter
1 tablespoon honey
1 teaspoon sambal oelek
2 tablespoons chinese rice wine
1 tablespoon fresh lemon juice

Combine all ingredients except chicken and stir until combined. Slice chicken breasts into bite-size pieces and place in marinade for 2-4 hours. Thread 4 or 5 pieces on to long wooden skewers and cook over hot coals for about 5 minutes. Take care not to overcook. This sauce can be reduced (boiled gently until of sauce consistency) and served with the chicken.

BARBEQUED MARSHMALLOWS

Never waste hot coals — a marshmallow on the end of a wooden stick, grilled over hot coals is very appealing to kids (and big kids!).

FRESH FIGS IN BOURSIN SAUCE

5 large ripe figs
1 boursin cheese
1 tablespoon grapeseed oil
150 mls sour cream
pepper and salt

Place the boursin cheese and the oil in a food processor and mix until smooth and creamy. Add sour cream, salt and pepper to taste. Heat gently to warm. Cut figs into quarters and thread on wooden sticks. Sauce can be served warm or at room temperature, surrounded by figs for dipping.

PECAN PIE

Pastry:
250g unsalted butter
3 cups flour
1/2 cup icing sugar
pinch salt
2 egg yolks
1/2 cup pecans, ground

Sift flour, salt and sugar together. Combine with the softened butter in a food processor, or by hand. Add egg and combine. Stir in the pecans. Wrap in plastic and chill. When ready to use, roll out on a lightly floured board. Use to line a 20cm spring form pan. Allow to rest for 1/2 hour.

Filling:
60g butter
1 cup brown sugar
1/2 teaspoon pure vanilla
pinch salt
3 eggs
1/2 cup light corn syrup
1 tablespoon plain flour
1 cup pecan nuts

Beat the butter, sugar, vanilla and salt until light and creamy. Add eggs, beating well after each addition. Add corn syrup and flour and mix well. Fold in the pecans and pour into prepared pastry case. Bake in a moderate oven for 25-30 minutes. Serve with lashings of double cream.

Fatty's Food For Thought:

MY FOUR SPECIAL BBQ GUESTS
1. Princess Diana — she looks like she needs a good time.
2. Simon O'Donnell — to provide the good time
3. Wilbur Smith — my favourite author. He'd be there to spin some yarns.
4. Local SP (essential) — so I can get on.

VEGGIES AND *Salads*

ZUCCHINI FRITTERS

3 medium zucchini
1/2 medium onion, finely chopped
2 eggs
pepper and salt
1 teaspoon lemon juice

Grate zucchini into a bowl. Using a fork, whisk the eggs and add the onion, lemon juice, pepper and salt. Combine this mixture with the zucchini. Spoon quantities of the mixture onto the oiled hotplate of the barbeque and cook for 1-2 minutes each side.

FRESH ASPARAGUS AND PARMESAN SALAD

1/2 cup grapeseed oil
2 tablespoons tarragon vinegar
1/2 teaspoon sugar
1/2 teaspoon powdered mustard
fresh tarragon
salt and freshly ground pepper
1 bunch asparagus, lightly cooked
fresh parmesan cheese
a selection of salad leaves eg. mignonette, white oak, chervil

Combine dressing ingredients and shake well. Toss salad leaves together and top with asparagus. Sprinkle liberally with the dressing and shaved parmesan cheese.

LEMON POTATOES

6 medium potatoes
2 tablespoons butter
juice of 1 lemon
salt and freshly ground pepper

Peel potatoes and cut into chunks. Melt butter in bottom of a baking tray and add potatoes. Sprinkle with salt and pepper and half lemon juice. Bake in a moderate oven for 15-20 'minutes, tossing occasionally. Sprinkle remainder of lemon over potatoes and cook for a further 10-15 minutes without turning. Serve immediately. Use the same method if cooking these potatoes in a covered barbeque.

PASTA SALAD

375g vegetable spiral pasta, cooked
2 tablespoons roasted pine nuts
2 tablespoons parmesan cheese, grated
100 mls grapeseed oil
1 tablespoon white wine vinegar
1 tablespoon lemon juice
2 tablespoons mixed fresh herbs, chopped eg. dill, basil, oregano, marjoram
2 cloves garlic, crushed
salt and pepper

Combine oil, vinegar, lemon juice, herbs, garlic, salt and pepper. Toss vinaigrette through the cooked pasta, with the parmesan cheese. Sprinkle with pine nuts and serve at room temperature.

SPINACH SALAD

1 bunch english or french spinach
1 tin water chestnuts, sliced
1 cup bean shoots
4-5 shallots, sliced
6 rashers bacon, chopped and fried

Dressing:
1/2 cup grapeseed oil
4 tablespoons vinegar
4 tablespoons spicy tomato sauce
2 tablespoons brown sugar
2 teaspoons worcestershire sauce
salt and freshly ground pepper

Wash and towel-dry the spinach. In a salad bowl place the spinach, bean shoots, drained and sliced water chestnuts, fried bacon pieces and chopped shallots. Toss together. To make the dressing, combine all ingredients in a screw top jar and shake well.

Veggies and Salads

PRAWN AND AVOCADO SALAD

large cooked prawns, peeled and de-veined
1 bunch watercress
1 avocado
1/4 cup chinese rice wine
1 teaspoon grapeseed oil
1/2 teaspoon hot sesame oil
1 teaspoon fish sauce
1 tablespoon shallots sliced
1 teaspoon lemongrass, white underlayer, finely sliced
1 teaspoon mint, chopped
1 teaspoon coriander, chopped

Combine all dressing ingredients, and leave to stand for at least an hour. Wash and dry watercress, add sliced avocado and prawns and shake the dressing over the salad. Serve.

GARLIC ROASTED TOMATOES

The best tomatoes to use for this recipe are the Italian "Roma" tomatoes, sometimes known as "egg tomatoes". Wash and dry tomatoes and core out the middle from the base end. Insert a leaf of basil and a clove of garlic into each tomato. Cook on barbeque hotplate for 15-20 minutes.

WARM POTATO SALAD WITH PINENUTS

1 kg baby new potatoes
your favourite vinaigrette (or sundried tomato vinaigrette — page 45)
1 spanish onion
roasted pinenuts

Gently boil unpeeled new potatoes, taking care not to let them split. Drain. While still warm sprinkle generously with vinaigrette of your choice, very finely sliced spanish onions and roasted pinenuts. Serve immediately.

Spicy crusted leg of lamb (p24)
with *Grilled, skewered chats* (p52)

BARBEQUED POTATO WEDGES

Peel and slice potatoes into wedges. Microwave for 5 minutes on high. Melt butter on the barbeque hotplate and toss potato wedges around until nicely golden (about 10-15 minutes). Serve with Bacon and Sour Cream Sauce (page 42) or Mango and Ginger Sauce (page 42).

CHERRY TOMATOES IN BALSAMIC VINEGAR

1 punnet firm, ripe cherry tomatoes
fresh basil
balsamic vinegar

Wash and dry cherry tomatoes and place in bowl. Tear basil leaves and sprinkle over tomatoes. Liberally douse tomatoes with balsamic vinegar.

BARBEQUED LEEK

4 leeks
lemon and parsley butter

Trim the tops of the leeks and peel. Cook leeks in the microwave for 2-3 minutes or sweat in pan with a little butter. Cut leeks in half lengthways and secure on skewers. To make lemon and parsley butter, chop 1 teaspoon of parsley and add to butter with 2 teaspoons of lemon juice. Roll into a cylinder shape, wrap in cling-wrap and return to refrigerator to firm. Cook leeks on the barbeque over a low heat, basting with the lemon and parsley butter.

Fatty's Food For Thought:
FAVOURITE MEALS
Two of my favourite meals include rice — beef stroganoff and chicken a la king. The missus has just about perfected these dishes. I honestly didn't know it was possible to burn rice by boiling it until I met her. Marriage can be a real learning experience.

A BIT ON THE *Side*

PARMESAN BREAD

1 french stick
200 g butter, room temperature
1-2 cups freshly grated parmesan cheese
1 heaped teaspoon oregano

Cut bread diagonally into slices and spread each side with butter. Mix grated parmesan and oregano in a bowl and dip one side of each bread slice into this mixture. Place cheese-side- up on a tray and bake in a moderate oven until bread is crisp.

CHEESE LOG

300 g table cheese
150 g butter
1/2 teaspoon hot mustard
2 teaspoons mustard seeds
2 teaspoons brandy

Grate cheese, soften butter, mix together. Add mustard, mustard seeds and brandy. Roll in toasted sesame seeds in shape of log. Serve with crackers or home-made croutons.

NOODLE CAKES

1 packet vermicelli rice noodles

Place in boiling water containing 1 tablespoon oil and cook until just tender. Drain. When cooked, place enough noodles to make a 6cm round cake on the barbeque hotplate — do not press down. Cook until the underside is nicely browned and use as the base for toppings of your choice, eg:

1. Serve under any kebabs with their marinade as a sauce;
2. Serve under a barbeque stir-fry (page 66) as a change from pita bread; or
3. Serve under roast garlic, eggplant and capsicum, with lamb juices poured over in recipe for Loin of Lamb (page 54).

Top: *Mixed mushroom salad* (p48)
Bottom: *Barbequed polenta with lemon and parmesan* (p36)

BARBEQUED POLENTA WITH LEMON AND PARMESAN

250 g polenta
1 cup cold water
1 1/2 — 2 cups boiling water
1 1/2 teaspoons salt
150 g stracchino
1 lemon
fresh parmesan cheese

Mix polenta and cold water. Add boiling water and salt and then cook for 10 minutes. Turn to a low heat and simmer for 15 minutes. Stir in stracchino. Place hot polenta into a greased tin and let stand until cold and solid. Cut into slices and fry until golden brown on both sides. Drain. Sprinkle with lemon juice and shaved fresh parmesan cheese. This polenta may also be served whole and round (photo page 35) if you have a suitable pan. Fry on both sides and serve on a platter with the lemon and parmesan.

BARBEQUED FOCACCIA PIZZAS

1 x 340g packet focaccia bread (available at supermarket delicatessens)

Spread with tomato puree and the topping of your choice, eg:
— salami, sliced spanish onion, chilli, roast capsicum and fresh mozzarella
— italian sausage, bacon, olives, fresh oregano and fresh mozzarella
— spanish salami, basil, sundried tomatoes, goats cheese, garlic and bocconcini
— mixed herbs, garlic, parmesan and fresh mozzarella

Place on barbeque over indirect heat with the lid down, for 5-10 minutes until base is crisp and cheese melted. Cook in covered barbeque the same way. On an open barbeque with no hood, place on a double piece of foil and cook over indirect heat. It may be necessary to place pizza under the grill for a minute or two.

Gourmet BARBIE

TRIM LAMB ROAST WITH PEAR AND PARMESAN

2 trimmed lamb roasts (approximately 300-350g each)
1/2 pear, peeled, cored and sliced
4 slices parmesan cheese
1/2 cup light olive oil
2 tablespoons red wine vinegar
2 tablespoons redcurrant jelly
2 tablespoons madeira
3 sprigs rosemary

Make a cavity through the middle of each roast and insert pieces of pear and parmesan cheese. Combine the oil, red wine vinegar, redcurrant jelly, madeira and rosemary. Place the lamb roasts in the marinade and allow to sit for at least 6 hours, turning from time to time. When ready to barbeque, place each roast in a piece of heavy duty foil (shiny side to the inside) and enclose. Cook over a moderate heat for approximately 30 minutes, or until tender. Remove from barbeque and allow to stand in foil for at least 20 minutes before serving. These roasts can be cooked without the foil, over indirect heat, on a hooded barbeque or any covered barbeque.

BEEF FILLET AND LEEK KEBAB

1 piece of beef fillet
1/4 cup green ginger wine
2 teaspoons japanese soy sauce
1 teaspoon sesame oil
1/2 teaspoon ginger, freshly grated
1 clove garlic
1 tablespoon sesame seeds
1 leek

Finely slice the beef fillet (it may be necessary to partly freeze the piece of beef before slicing), and lay in flat bottomed dish. Meanwhile, combine the green ginger wine, soy sauce, sesame oil, ginger, garlic and sesame seeds. Pour this marinade over the beef and leave for at least an hour. Trim leeks and cut the white section into 1/2 cm pieces. Separate the layers. Take a piece of the marinated beef, roll and thread on wooden skewer alternately with a piece of leek. Cook briefly on an oiled barbeque plate and serve at once. The remaining marinade can be reduced a little in a saucepan and served as a dipping sauce.

Left to right:
Paprika potatoes (p40),
Lemon potatoes (p28), Barbequed
potato wedges (p32), Stuffed potato skins (p106),
Honeyed sweet potatoes (p113), Tomato and
bocconcini salad (p24), Sour cream sauce with
mango and ginger (p42)

PAPRIKA POTATOES

1 kg potatoes
60 g butter
4 shallots
salt and freshly ground pepper
1 cup sour cream
1 tablespoon paprika

Peel, wash and dry potatoes. Cut into quarters or wedges. Heat in butter in large baking tray. Add potatoes and cook at 180, turning occasionally. When potatoes are tender and lightly golden brown, add chopped shallots, salt and pepper and cook for a few minutes longer. Combine sour cream and paprika and add to potatoes, stirring lightly. Cover and heat gently.

FRESH FRUIT WITH MASCARPONE

Choose a selection of fresh fruits eg. strawberries, kiwi fruit, mangos, lychees, rockmelon
Mascarpone:
250g mascarpone
2 tablespoons sugar
2 tablespoons brandy
1/2 cup cream
2 egg whites

In a mixer whisk together the mascarpone, sugar, brandy and cream. Fold in the beaten eggwhites. Serve surrounded by fresh fruits.

Fatty's Food For Thought:

THE IDEAL BARBIE
The first rule is to avoid having barbeques at places where you have to indulge in strenuous exercise such as touch footy, baseball or cricket. On a stinking hot day, there is only one place to have a barbie — around the pool at home. You can relax, keep cool, have a swim and maybe even get pushed in fully-clothed and discover your expensive Swiss watch isn't waterproof after all, despite what they said in Zurich.

SOMETHING *Saucy*

SWEET CHILLI SAUCE

1/4 cup white wine vinegar
1/4 cup sugar
1-2 small red chillis, finely sliced
1 teaspoon fish sauce
2 teaspoons fresh coriander, chopped
finely diced cucumber

Combine all ingredients and leave to stand, preferably overnight.

To make a very tangy vinaigrette, just add 1/4 cup of oil to the Sweet Chilli Sauce.

SOUR CREAM SAUCE WITH MANGO AND GINGER

1/2 cup sour cream
2 tablespoons mango and ginger chutney
2 teaspoons sambal oelek
2 teaspoons lemon juice

Combine all ingredients and use with barbequed white meats.

BACON AND SOUR CREAM SAUCE

300mls sour cream
3 rashers bacon
1/2 medium onion, chopped
3 sundried tomatoes
good dash tabasco

Chop bacon into small pieces and toss in a pan with the onion, over a medium heat, until golden and crisp. Drain. Add to the sour cream with the sundried tomatoes and a good dash (or two) of tabasco.

Juggling these is easy, but how do they get them into the sauce bottle?

SPICY TOMATO SAUCE

1 tin pureed tomatoes
1 tablespoon butter
1 small onion, grated
1 teaspoon sugar
1/4 cup red wine
1/4 cup water
3-4 basil leaves
1 small hot chilli, sliced
freshly ground black pepper

Melt the butter in a heavy pan and saute onion for 2-3 minutes. Add tomato puree, sugar, red wine, water, basil leaves, chilli and pepper. Simmer gently for 15-20 minutes, until sauce has thickened a little.

GARLIC OIL

To 1/4 cup of light olive oil, add 2 cloves crushed garlic and a little freshly ground black pepper. Leave for 24 hours before using. Keep refrigerated. Handy to have as a baste to add flavour to any red meat.

CURRY YOGHURT SAUCE

200g plain yoghurt
1 teaspoon good curry powder
1 teaspoon paprika
1 teaspoon powdered ginger
2 teaspoons brown sugar
2 teaspoons lemon juice
salt and pepper

Combine all ingredients and allow to stand for at least an hour or two before serving.

RED CAPSICUM VINAIGRETTE

2 ripe red capsicums and 1 tablespoon oil
2/3 cup light olive oil
1/4 cup good white wine vinegar
1 clove garlic, chopped
a little sugar
salt and freshly ground black pepper

Place whole capsicums, brushed with olive oil on a tray in a hot oven. When seared all over (about 20 mins) remove from oven, allow to cool a little and skin the capsicums, removing seeds, stems and membranes. Puree in a blender. Combine light olive oil, vinegar, garlic, sugar, salt and pepper to make vinaigrette. Blend in the pureed capsicum to a smooth consistency. Store in refrigerator.

MINT AND CORIANDER SAUCE

1 small carton yoghurt
1 tablespoon fresh coriander
1 tablespoon fresh mint
1 teaspoon sugar
1 tablespoon tamarind sauce or lemon juice
1 teaspoon ground cumin

Mix all ingredients together and allow to stand, preferably and hour or more. Serve.

SUNDRIED TOMATO VINAIGRETTE

1/2 cup sundried tomato oil (drained from a jar of sundried tomatoes)
4 tablespoons balsamic vinegar
2 teaspoons sugar — a little more if you prefer a sweeter dressing
2 sprigs rosemary
salt and freshly ground black pepper

Combine the sundried tomato oil, balsamic vinegar, sugar, salt and pepper. When well combined, place the rosemary in the oil and allow to infuse for at least 24 hours. Use to dress salads, especially when serving lamb.

Sauces, Marinades and Dressings

Just a little something I cooked up

AFTER THE *Game*

OLIVE FOCACCIA WITH HERBED OLIVE OIL

1 piece of olive focaccia bread (if unavailable, plain focaccia is fine)
200 ml pure virgin olive oil
1 heaped teaspoon fresh oregano
1 heaped teaspoon fresh basil
1 heaped teaspoon fresh rosemary
1 heaped teaspoon fresh marjoram
2 cloves garlic, crushed
juice 1 lemon
coarse salt and freshly ground black pepper

Cut focaccia into finger slices. Finely chop the fresh herbs and add to oil with the garlic. Whisk until flavours combine. Add lemon, salt and black pepper and whisk again. Serve surrounded by focaccia for dipping.

SPICY GARLIC PRAWNS

20 green king prawns
1/4 cup mustardseed oil
1/4 cup green ginger wine
1 teaspoon freshly grated ginger
3 cloves garlic, crushed
1/2 teaspoon chilli powder

Mix together the marinade ingredients. Peel and de-vein prawns. leaving on the tails. Place prawns in the marinade and leave for 3-4 hours. Thread 2 or 3 prawns on a wooden skewer and barbeque for a few minutes until just cooked.

MIXED MUSHROOM SALAD

1/2 cup olive oil
2 tablespoons red wine vinegar
1 teaspoon sugar
1 clove garlic, sliced
2 teaspoons continental parsley
a selection of fresh mushrooms eg. button, oyster, swiss brown, white coral or golden
a variety of lettuce leaves eg. lambs tongue, butter and radicchio

Combine ingredients for vinaigrette and shake well. Toss salad leaves with mushrooms. When ready to serve sprinkle liberally with the vinaigrette.

Olive focaccia with herbed olive oil (p48)

STANDING RIB ROAST *(Serves 6)*

rib roast on the bone, about 2kg (ask your butcher to trim the bones and truss the meat)
1/2 bottle red wine
2 tablespoons olive oil
1 medium onion, sliced
1 medium carrot, chopped
1 stick celery, chopped
2 bay leaves
2 cloves garlic, crushed
1 teaspoon mustard seed
salt and freshly ground black pepper

Combine all ingredients for the marinade. Pour over the standing rib roast and marinate for several hours, turning to make sure all meat reaches marinade. Place the meat on the barbeque and cook over indirect heat under a roasting hood for 1-1 1/2 hours. Once or twice during cooking, meat can be brushed with garlic oil. Allow meat to stand for 10-15 minutes before serving. Strain remaining marinade, reduce and serve over ribs. This recipe works well on the covered barbeque.

TASTY BARBEQUED ONIONS

4 medium onions
60 g butter
2 teaspoons sugar
oyster sauce

Slice onions and saute on barbeque with butter and sugar until slightly caramelised. Sprinkle oyster sauce over onions and toss through until cooked.

Fatty's Food For Thought:

FOUR PEOPLE I WOULDN'T INVITE TO A BARBIE
1. Prince Charles — how boring
2. Idi Amin — he might want to throw me on if we had underestimated the number of snags needed.
3. Any politician — you don't need me to tell you why.
4. Jack the Ripper — although I suppose the knife could be handy if we were a bit short in the cutlery department.

TABLE FOR *Two*

LOIN OF LAMB WITH ROASTED GARLIC, EGGPLANT AND CAPSICUM *(Serves 4-6)*

1 kg eye of loin of lamb (sold as trim lamb in butchers)
1 teaspoon ground cumin
1 teaspoon ground coriander
salt and freshly ground black pepper
garlic or mustard seed oil
4 whole heads of garlic
eggplant (see Mozarella and Eggplant Bake page 52)
roast capsicum (see Roast Capsicum and Fennel page 52)

Place the whole garlics in individual pieces of foil, drizzle with a little olive oil and place on the barbeque over indirect heat for about 30 minutes until cooked. Mix the herbs with the salt and pepper. Brush the loins of lamb with the oil and press the seasoning into either side. Grill on hotplate for approximately 3-5 minutes each side. The outside should be quite firm and coloured and the inside soft and pink. Serve the lamb and garlic with the eggplant and roast capsicum.

TROUT CUTLET WITH GINGER AND LIME BUTTER

4 ocean trout cutlets, 2-2 1/2 cm thick
light sesame oil
ginger and lime butter

To make ginger and lime butter: To 50 g of softened butter add 1 teaspoon of lime juice and 1 teaspoon of finely grated ginger and combine evenly. Roll into a cylinder shape and wrap in cling wrap and refrigerate until firm.

Lightly oil a moderately hot barbeque plate with light sesame oil. Cook cutlets on one side for 2-3 minutes. Turn and brush liberally with ginger and lime butter. Cook each side of the cutlets for 2-3 minutes — fish should remain quite a deep pink inside. Take off the hot plate and brush the second side liberally with the ginger lime butter. Serve with a sprinkling of freshly ground black pepper.

Loin of lamb (p52) with
Eggplant and mozarella bake (p54),
Roast capsicum (p143) and *Garlic tomatoes* (p30)

EGGPLANT AND MOZZARELLA BAKES

1 eggplant
1 bulb mozzarella cheese
fresh basil leaves (optional)

Slice eggplant into 1/2 cm rounds and top with slightly smaller round of mozzarella. If using basil, place one or two basil leaves between eggplant and cheese. Place on hot barbeque and cook, without turning, until eggplant is just cooked and cheese is melting.

GRILLED SKEWERED CHATS

1/2 kg baby new potatoes
3 tablespoons peanut oil
1 tablespoon lemon juice
coarsely gound salt and pepper

Par-boil unpeeled potatoes to just tender. Thread 3 or 4 potatoes onto the end of wooden skewers, which have been soaked in water for several hours or overnight. Combine oil, lemon juice, salt and pepper. Place skewered potatoes on barbeque and brush with oil mixture. Cook for 5-10 minutes, turning often and continuing to brush with the mixture.

ROAST CAPSICUM AND FENNEL

red and green capsicum
1 bulb fennel
garlic oil

Cut capsicum in half, de-seed and trim pith. Slice lengthways into 3-4cm strips and cut each strip into 3. Thread onto the end of long wooden skewers. Trim fennel and cut into a similar size. Thread onto skewers. You may wish to alternate capsicum and fennel on the one skewer. Brush vegetables on both sides with garlic oil. Place on hotplate of the barbeque over a medium-low heat and cook for approximately 20 minutes, brushing with garlic oil and turning frequently.

SIMPLY STRAWBERRIES

A lovely way to finish a barbeque is to simply take a punnet of strawberries (do not wash or hull), and sprinkle liberally with balsamic vinegar. Serve with King Island Cream or clotted cream.

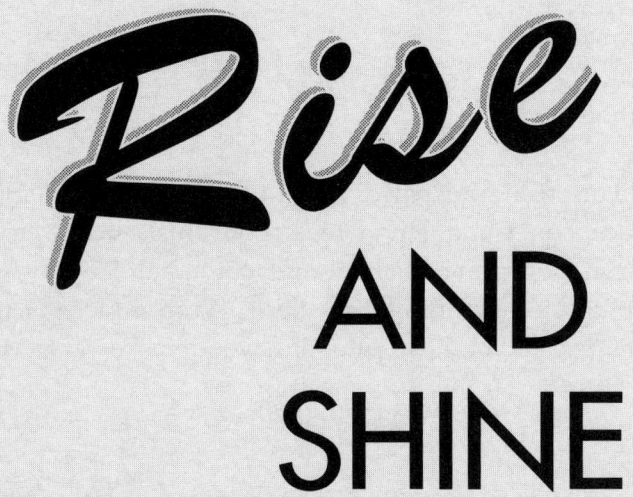

FRESH FRUIT PLATTER WITH FRUITY SAUCE

2 cups apple juice
1/2 cup green ginger wine

Combine apple juice and green ginger wine in a saucepan and simmer over a moderate heat until mixture has reduced to 1/2 cup. Serve sprinkled over a platter of fresh fruit.

GLAZED CHICKEN LIVERS AND BACON

9 chicken livers
6 rashers bacon
1 tablespoon soy sauce
1 tablespoon honey
1 tablespoon lemon juice

Rinse chicken livers well and pat dry. Cut each side of double liver in half. In a bowl, combine soy sauce, honey and lemon juice. Pour this sauce over the chicken livers. Marinate for 1-2 hours. Trim the bacon rashers of rind, cut in half lengthways then cut each length into three. (6 wrapping pieces from each rasher.) Wrap a piece of bacon around each piece of chicken liver and thread 3 of these onto long wooden skewers. Makes 12 skewers.

MARINATED LAMB NOISETTES

4 x eye of loin of lamb (can use veal fillet)
8 rashers bacon
1/4 cup grapeseed oil
2 cloves garlic
1 small onion, chopped
1/4 cup dry vermouth
1 tablespoon fresh mint
freshly grated black pepper

Cut lamb or veal into 5cm pieces and turn on end. Meanwhile, combine oil, garlic, onion, vermouth, mint and pepper and pour over the small noisettes of lamb. Leave to marinate for at least 4 hours. Cut rind off bacon and cut each rasher in half. When ready to barbeque wrap a piece of bacon around each noisette and secure with a toothpick. Cook on hot plate 3-4 minutes each side.

Marinated lamb noisettes (p56) with Country style omlette and French toast (p58)

FRENCH TOAST

4 slices bread
1/2 cup milk
2 eggs
salt and pepper
butter

Mix together the milk, eggs, salt and pepper. Melt the butter on the hotplate of the barbeque. Dip both sides of the bread into the egg mixture and cook in the butter until golden and crispy. Serve with Country Style Omelette (below).

COUNTRY STYLE OMELETTE

6 eggs
3 tablespoons water
180g italian sausage, chopped into chunks
3 rashers bacon, sliced
1 small onion, sliced
chunks of pre-cooked (or left over) potatoes
3-4 sundried tomatoes, chopped
1 tablespoon continental parsley
freshly ground pepper
1 tablespoon butter

In a large bowl, beat the eggs with the water. Add all the other ingredients except the butter and mix through. Place a heavy pan on the barbeque over moderate heat and melt the butter. Add the egg mixture and cook slowly allowing the omelette to set. Towards the end of cooking, place a cover over the pan to set the top of the omelette. Serve immediately with hot damper (page 12) or french toast (above). Serve flat, do not try to fold omelette.

GLAZED HAM STEAKS

4 ham steaks
2 tablespoons honey
1 teaspoon dijon mustard
1 tablespoon dry sherry
1 teaspoon soy sauce
few drops lemon juice

Combine all basting ingredients and brush over steaks. Cook briefly on the barbeque, basting frequently.

Snags GALORE

CHILLI AND PINEAPPLE SAUSAGES

Par-boil thick beef sausages or cook in microwave for 3 minutes on high. Drain thoroughly. Split lengthways for pocket. Spread a little hot chilli sauce inside and place enough pineapple to fill the pocket. Secure with a toothpick. Then place on the barbeque and cook for a further 10-15 minutes.

GARLIC AND MUSHROOM SAUSAGES

Par-boil thick beef sausages or cook in microwave for 3 minutes on high. Drain thoroughly. Split lengthways for pocket. Meanwhile, slice fresh mushrooms. Add freshly crushed garlic and saute for 1-2 minutes in a little butter. Fill the pocket with mushroom mixture and secure with toothpicks. Then place on the barbeque and cook for a further 10-15 minutes.

PRUNE AND BACON SAUSAGES

Par-boil thick beef sausages or cook in microwave for 3 minutes on high. Drain thoroughly. Split lengthways for pocket. Place a pitted prune in each pocket and wrap sausages with bacon. Secure with toothpicks. Place on barbeque and cook for a further 10-15 minutes.

PEANUT AND BACON SAUSAGES

Par-boil thick beef sausages or cook in microwave for 3 minutes on high. Drain thoroughly. Split lengthways for pocket. Spread inside pocket with peanut butter. Wrap sausage with bacon and secure with toothpick. Place on barbeque and cook for a further 10-15 minutes. A tasty alternative is to sprinke a little tobasco on peanut butter before wrapping with bacon.

APPLE AND HONEY SAUSAGES

Par-boil thick beef sausages or cook in microwave for 3 minutes on high. Drain thoroughly. Split lengthways for pocket. Peel and core granny smith apple and cut into slices. Sprinkle with lemon juice and drizzle with honey. Fill cavity of sausages with apple pieces and secure with a toothpick. Place on barbeque and cook for a further 10-15 minutes.

Assorted sausages
(pp 60 and 62)

KRANSKY WITH MUSTARD AND STRACCHINO

Slice kransky lengthways to form pocket and spread with a little hot mustard (you can use french mustard if you prefer). Place a slice of stracchino cheese in the pocket and secure with a toothpick. Place on barbeque and cook for 10-15 minutes.

GREEK FLAVOURED SAUSAGES

Par-boil thick beef sausages or cook on microwave for 3 minutes on high. Drain thoroughly. Split lengthways for pocket. Chop fresh oregano and mint, and sprinkle inside pocket. Place a slice of halloumi cheese (available from cheese shops and delicatessens) in with the herbs and secure with toothpicks. Place on barbeque and cook for a further 10-15 minutes.

ITALIAN STYLE SAUSAGES

Par-boil thick beef sausages or cook in microwave for 3 minutes on high. Drain thoroughly. Split lengthwise for pocket. Spread inside with sundried tomato puree, a little (or a lot!) of grated garlic and 2-3 fresh basil leaves. Secure with a toothpick. Place on barbeque and cook for a further 10-15 minutes.

CARPET BAG SAUSAGES

Par-boil thick beef sausages or cook in microwave for 3 minutes on high. Split lengthways for pocket. Take a spoonful of Carpet Bag filling (see recipe page 68) and use to fill pocket. Secure with a toothpick, place on the barbeque and cook for a further 10-15 minutes.

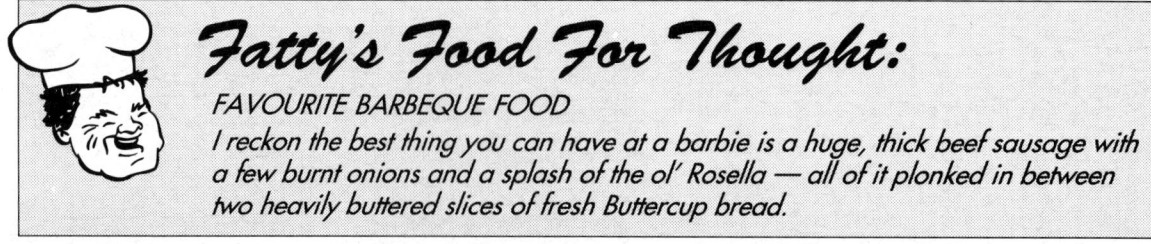

Fatty's Food For Thought:

FAVOURITE BARBEQUE FOOD
I reckon the best thing you can have at a barbie is a huge, thick beef sausage with a few burnt onions and a splash of the ol' Rosella — all of it plonked in between two heavily buttered slices of fresh Buttercup bread.

BIG 'N Beefy

Luscious lamb shanks (p76) with *Baby golden nugget pumpkin* (p10) and *Herbed flowerpot bread* (p24)

TANGY PEPPER STEAK

4 beef steaks, either rump, t-bone or scotch fillet
freshly ground black peppercorns
1 tablespoon butter
1/4 cup dry sherry
2 tablespoons tomato paste
sour cream to taste

Lightly oil the base of a heavy pan and place on the hottest part of the barbeque. Press peppercorns into both sides of steaks and cook in pan until tender. Remove steaks and set aside. Add to the pan the butter, dry sherry, tomato paste and sour cream, stirring until consistency thickens a little. Pour over steaks and serve immediately.

HERBED TRIM LAMB ROAST *(Serves 4)*

2 trimmed lamb roasts (approximately 300-350g each)
1/4 cup jasmine rice, cooked
1 teaspoon fresh mint, chopped
1 teaspoon fresh coriander, chopped
1 tablespoon roasted pine nuts
salt and freshly ground pepper

Combine the rice, herbs, nuts, salt and pepper.

1/2 cup grapeseed oil
2 cloves garlic, sliced
2 small red chillies, sliced
2 teaspoons coriander, chopped
2 teaspoons mint, chopped
2 teaspoons fish sauce
2 tablespoons lime juice
3-4 lime leaves, crushed

Make a cavity through the middle of each roast and fill with rice mixture. Combine oil, garlic, chillies, coriander, mint, fish sauce, lime juice and lime leaves. Place the lamb roasts in the marinade and allow to sit for at least 6 hours, turning from time to time. When ready to barbeque, place each roast in a piece of heavy duty foil (shiny side to the inside) and enclose. Cook over a moderate heat for approximately 30 minutes or until tender. Remove from barbeque and allow to stand in foil for at least 20 minutes before serving. These roasts can be cooked without the foil, over indirect heat, on a hooded barbeque or any covered barbeque.

BARBEQUE STIR-FRY BEEF FOR PITA BREAD

600g beef fillet
1 medium onion, sliced
1/2 red capsicum
1/2 green capsicum
soy bean curd (optional)
fresh bamboo shoots
1 packet small pita pockets or lavash bread

Marinade:
2 tablespoons soy sauce
2 tablespoons blackbean sauce
2 cloves garlic, crushed
1/2 teaspoons chinese five spice
4 tablespoons vegetable oil

Cut beef fillet into strips approximately 6cm long. Combine all marinade ingredients and pour over beef. Marinate for 2-4 hours. Meanwhile, slice onions, remove seeds and pith from capsicums then slice. Cut soya bean curd (if using) into cubes approximately 1 1/2cm. Lightly oil hot plate of barbeque and over a moderate heat cook onions, capsicums, soya bean and beef. This also works well in a heavy pan over a grill plate. Toss through with a little of the marinade for a few minutes, until beef is just cooked and vegetables are still crunchy. Place inside pita pocket or roll in lavash bread along with fresh bean shoots.

BACON BURGERS

500 g minced beef — not too lean — it is important that the burger stay moist
6 rashers bacon, rind removed
1 medium onion, finely chopped
1 egg, whisked
120 g cheddar cheese, grated
1 egg
grated rind 1/2 lemon
salt and freshly ground black pepper

Chop bacon into small pieces and saute in pan until almost cooked. Add chopped onion and cook until transparent. In the meantime, combine all other ingredients. Remove bacon and onion from heat and add to meat mixture. Form into burgers and cook on hot plate of barbeque until just cooked.

Barbeque beef stir-fry and pita bread (p66)

CARPET BAG STEAKS

Choose thick cuts of beef for this dish to enable a pocket to be cut deep enough to take the filling. Suggested cuts are scotch fillet, rump and t-bone.

Filling:
1 bottle oysters, drained and roughly chopped
125 g mushrooms, chopped
1/2 cup breadcrumbs
1 tablespoon chopped fresh oregano
1 tablespoon chopped fresh parsley
grated rind 1/2 lemon
garlic salt
freshly ground pepper
50 g butter

Place butter in saucepan over heat and add all filling ingredients, except oysters. Gently fry for a few minutes and remove from heat. Add oysters and set aside to cool. Place mixture in pockets of steaks and secure with toothpicks. Grill steaks in the usual way on your barbeque.

MARINATED NECK CHOPS

1 kg lamb neck chops
1 tin tomato pieces
1/2 cup white wine
4 tablespoons oil
2 tablespoons honey
1/2 cup fresh mint, chopped
2 cloves garlic, sliced
1 small onion, chopped
1 teaspoon worcestershire sauce

Place tinned tomato pieces in a baking dish and mash with a potato masher. Add wine, oil, honey, mint, garlic, onion and worcestershire sauce. Trim chops of fat and place in marinade for at least 4 hours. Double fold several pieces of heavy duty foil (shiny side to the inside) and place 3-4 chops on each piece. Spoon marinade over the chops and close the foil securely. Cook on the barbeque over a medium heat for at least an hour until tender. Take care when unwrapping the parcels not to lose the juices. Serve these juices over the chops.

PORK NECK STUFFED WITH PRUNES

This is a very economical piece of meat as it has no bones and a minimum of fat.
1 kg piece of pork neck
1 packet of pitted prunes
walnut oil (or oil of your choice)

With a knife steel or similar object make a long cavity lengthways through the pork neck. From each end stuff prunes towards the middle, filling the cavity. Brush with walnut oil and place on a double sheet of heavy duty foil (shiny side to the inside) and fold to enclose meat securely. Cook on barbeque over moderate heat for 3/4 — 1 hour until cooked. Allow to stand for at least 10 minutes before carving. Reserve juices contained in foil and serve over pork. Serve with Paprika Potatoes (page 40).
This recipe works well in the covered barbeque.

BEEF CHILLI BURGERS

500 g minced beef — not too lean — it is important that the burger stay moist
1 teaspoon red curry paste
1 egg, whisked
4 tablespoons spicy red sauce
1 teaspoon sugar
ground black pepper and salt

Mix all ingredients together and shape into patties. Sprinkle hot plate of barbeque with hot chilli/sesame oil and cook burgers until just cooked.

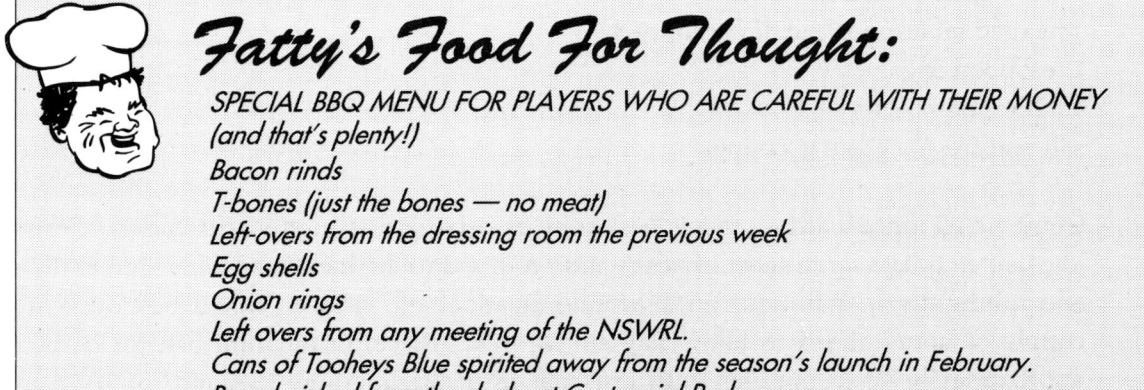

Fatty's Food For Thought:
SPECIAL BBQ MENU FOR PLAYERS WHO ARE CAREFUL WITH THEIR MONEY
(and that's plenty!)
Bacon rinds
T-bones (just the bones — no meat)
Left-overs from the dressing room the previous week
Egg shells
Onion rings
Left overs from any meeting of the NSWRL.
Cans of Tooheys Blue spirited away from the season's launch in February.
Bread nicked from the ducks at Centennial Park.

Big 'n Beefy

FOUR PEPPERCORN STEAK

choose rump, t-bone or scotch fillet
mustard oil
black, white, pink and green peppercorns (available as "Peppercorn Blend" at gourmet delicatessens or large department stores)

Steaks should be approximately 2 1/2 cm thick. Brush steaks with oil and press coarsely cracked peppercorns into both sides of each steak about an hour before cooking. Cook to your liking on hot oiled plate of barbeque, or over hot, glowing coals.

Remember: — firm outside but soft to touch gives rare steak.
— firm outside but springy to touch gives medium-rare; and
— firm is well done.

MEATLOAF

500g mince
1 cup soft breadcrumbs
1/4 cup red wine
1/4 cup tomato puree
1/2 medium onion, chopped
1 egg, well beaten
1 clove garlic, crushed
1 heaped tablespoon parsley, chopped
1 teaspoon sugar
1 tablespoon butter
salt and freshly ground pepper

Combine all ingredients — this is best done by mixing thoroughly with hands. Form into a **log shape.** Fold a large sheet of heavy duty foil to double thickness (shiny side to the inside) **and rub lightly with butter.** Wrap around meatloaf and secure. This is best done at least a **couple of hours ahead** to allow flavours to mix. Place on medium heat of barbeque for **approximately 40-45 minutes** until just cooked through. Allow to stand for 10-15 minutes **before cutting.** Serve with Spicy Tomato Sauce (page 44).

Four peppercorn steak (p70)

BASTED LAMB LOIN CHOPS WITH KIDNEYS *(Serves 4)*

8 lamb loin chops, at least 2 1/2cm thick (ask butcher to leave tails long)
4 lambs kidneys
fresh basil and oregano
1 small onion, finely chopped
3 tablespoons light olive oil
1 tablespoon red wine vinegar
2 tablespoons worcestershire sauce
1/2 cup spicy tomato sauce
1/2 teaspoon dried basil
1/2 teaspoon dried oregano
salt and freshly ground pepper

To make baste: Place onion, oil, vinegar, worcestershire sauce, spicy tomato sauce, dried herbs, salt and pepper in a saucepan and cook for 10 minutes.

Open out tail of lamb chops and trim of fat. Sprinkle with a little chopped fresh basil and oregano and brush with baste. Pull away membrane from kidneys and cut lengthways through side. With pointed knife remove the fatty core of the kidney. Place a half kidney on each opened-out chop so that tail of chop wraps around to secure kidney. Fasten tail with wooden skewer or strong toothpick. Sit chops in baste mixture an hour before cooking, turning once. Seal chops over hot grill on both sides and around tail. Reduce heat to moderate and cook chops until done to your liking, continuing to baste whilst cooking.

CHILLI BBQ LAMB CHOPS *(Serves 4)*

4 large barbeque chops
2 tablespoons peanut butter
2 tablespoons sweet chilli sauce
1 tablespoon water

Mix together peanut butter, sweet chilli sauce and water. Barbeque chops until done on one side. Turn. While other side is cooking, spread with peanut and chilli mixture. Do not turn again. This gives the chops a really interesting flavour.

BEEF STEAKS WITH SEASONED BUTTER *(Serves 4)*

4 pieces of steak — scotch fillet, rump or t-bone at least 2 1/2cm thick
100g butter
1 tablespoon mustard seeds
1 tablespoon mixed peppercorns (available as "Peppercorn Blend")
1 teaspoon dijon mustard

Bring butter to room temperature and blend in mustard seeks, mixed peppercorns and mustard. Roll into a cylinder shape and chill. Prepare the steaks by cutting a pocket, well into the centre of the beef, and place slices of seasoned butter into each pocket. Seal pocket and cook over hot coals, so that the meat is quite crispy on the outside but soft and tender on the inside. Serve with a pat of the seasoned butter on top.

FRUITY GLAZED PORK CHOPS

4 pork loin chops or butterfly pork chops
2 tablespoons plum jam
2 tablespoons apricot jam
1 teaspoon hoi sin sauce
2 teaspoons lemon juice
2 tablespoons dry sherry

Combine all ingredients and gently heat until jams are melted. Cool. Pour over pork and leave to marinate for approximately 1 hour. Cook over hot coals on the barbeque hotplate. Cook for 3-4 minutes on either side, depending on thickness of chop. Baste frequently with marinade. Use remaining marinade as sauce on chops.

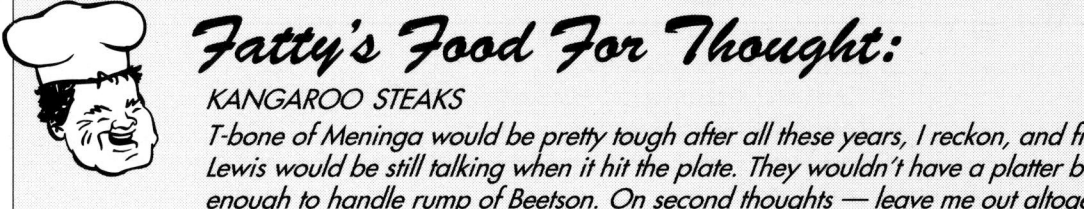

Fatty's Food For Thought:
KANGAROO STEAKS
T-bone of Meninga would be pretty tough after all these years, I reckon, and fillet of Lewis would be still talking when it hit the plate. They wouldn't have a platter big enough to handle rump of Beetson. On second thoughts — leave me out altogether!

SWEET TOMATO PORK RIBS *(Serves 4)*

1kg thick pork ribs (also works well with pork loin chops)
100g tomato paste
1/2 cup water
2 tablespoons hoi sin sauce
2 tablespoons honey
2 tablespoons vegetable oil
1 teaspoon fresh ginger, grated
2 cloves garlic, crushed

Mix together all ingredients. Place the ribs or chops into the marinade and allow to stand for at least 4 hours. Cook on the barbeque, basting with the marinade.

MARINATED LAMB CUTLETS

8 lamb cutlets, trimmed of fat
1 small onion, finely chopped
1 clove garlic, crushed
1/2 cup chopped fresh mint
2 tablespoons honey
4 tablespoons oil
1/2 cup white wine
freshly ground black pepper

Mix all marinade ingredients together, then pour over the cutlets and leave to marinate in the fridge for at least 4 hours, or overnight. Place on a hot grill and cook for a few minutes, turning once. Do not overcook — cutlets should still be pink when cut.

Fatty's Food For Thought:

BREAKFAST BARBIE
1. Orange juice (vodka optional).
2. Corn Flakes and Tooheys.
3. Toast and Vegemite (or marmalade) and Tooheys.
4. Cup of Tooheys (no sugar).
5. Tomorrow's race results (to help with strategic plan for the day at friendly local TAB Agency).

Preparation for *Marinated lamb cutlets* (p74)

LUSCIOUS LAMB SHANKS

4 lamb shanks
120 mls olive oil
2 cloves garlic, crushed
1 teaspoon ground oregano
2 teaspoons ground rosemary
50 mls red wine vinegar
salt and freshly ground pepper
fresh oregano and rosemary

Place lamb shanks in a bowl and combine all ingredients except the fresh herbs. Roll shanks in this mixture and leave to stand for at least 2 hours. Take 4 large, doubled sheets of heavy duty foil (shiny side to the inside). Place one shank on each piece of foil. Pour the remaining marinade over the shanks. Add fresh rosemary and oregano to each and fold up to form a securely closed packet. Place on a moderately hot barbeque and cook for approximately 1 hour.

Tasty Barbequed Onions (page 48) go well with this meal.

BARBEQUED RACKS OF LAMB *(Serves 4)*

2 racks of lamb (6 cutlets each)
3/4 cup grapeseed oil
1/3 cup apple juice
1 tablespoon redcurrant jelly
2 cloves garlic
3-4 sprigs fresh rosemary
salt and freshly cracked black pepper

Trim excess fat from racks of lamb, leaving about 5cm of bone exposed. Mix together grapeseed oil, apple juice, redcurrant jelly, garlic, rosemary, salt and pepper. Place lamb racks in a dish and pour over the marinade. Leave overnight or all day, turning occasionally. Remove from the marinade and wrap in a large piece of heavy duty (shiny side to the inside) and cook on moderate heat of barbeque for 20 minutes. Remove from foil, cook for a further 10-15 minutes, brushing frequently with remainder of marinade. Combine juices from the foil with some of the remaining marinade, heat and serve with the lamb.

GONE Fishin'

HONEY AND WALNUT CUTLETS *

4-6 fish cutlets of your choice
1/2 cup honey
1/3 cup walnut oil
1/3 cup teriyaki sauce
3 cloves garlic, crushed
1/4 teaspoon pepper

Combine honey, oil, teriyaki, garlic and pepper. Mix well until combined. Add cutlets. Marinate for 2-4 hours, or overnight. Drain. Place onto a well-greased barbeque plate or grill. Cook for approximately 3-4 minutes on each side, basting frequently with marinade.

ORANGE GINGER CUTLETS *

4-6 fish cutlets of your choice
3/4 cup orange juice
1 tablespoon grated orange rind
1/2 cup golden syrup
1/3 cup ginger wine
1 tablespoon ginger, chopped

Combine orange juice, rind, golden syrup, ginger wine and ginger. Mix until well combined. Add cutlets. Marinate for 2-4 hours, or overnight. Drain. Place onto a well-greased barbeque plate or grill. Cook for approximately 3-4 minutes on each side, basting frequently with marinade.

TANGY VERMOUTH CUTLETS *

4-6 fish cutlets of your choice
1/3 cup vermouth
1/3 cup lime or lemon juice
1/4 cup oil
1 tablespoon parsley, chopped
1 teaspoon lime or lemon rind, grated
1/4 teaspoon pepper

Combine vermouth, lime or lemon juice, oil, parsley, rind and pepper. Mix until well combined. Add cutlets. Marinate for 2-4 hours, or overnight. Drain. Place onto a well-greased barbeque plate or grill. Cook for approximately 3-4 minutes on each side, basting frequently with marinade.

In dish: *Blue eye cutlets in orange and ginger marinade.*
Out of dish: *Jewfish cutlets with tangy vermouth marinade* (p78)

SPICY MARINATED MULLET *

750 g mullet fillets
1 medium onion, finely chopped
1 x 2 cm piece fresh ginger, finely grated
1 clove garlic, crushed
1/4 cup cider vinegar
3 tablespoons dry sherry
3 drops tabasco sauce

Combine the marinade ingredients in a bowl and mix well. Lay mullet fillets into a shallow dish and pour the marinade over. Cover and place into the refrigerator and allow mullet to marinate for approximately 2 hours. Prepare barbeque to a medium heat and oil the plate or grill. Place fillets over heat and cook for approximately 3 minutes each side. Turn only once during cooking.

BARBEQUED OCTOPUS *

500 g small octopus
1/2 cup olive oil
1/4 cup lemon juice
1 clove garlic, crushed
2 tablespoons parsley, finely chopped

Clean octopus by cutting vertically through one side of the head and tentacles. Remove sacs from the head and the "beak" (this is a hard shell piece located at the centre where the tentacles join), discard these parts. Wash octopus under clean water. Combine olive oil, lemon juice, garlic and parsley — mix well. Place octopus onto barbeque plate and brush generously with marinade. Cook for approximately 10 minutes.

Note: The octopus will curl and then turn a claret red colour, which looks most attractive in a garden salad. Occasionally even the small octopus can be tough. You can tenderise before cooking by steaming for approximately 4-5 minutes.

FAVOURITE BBQ SPOT
In a country like Australia there are plenty of nice places to set up the barbie, but one that's really hard to toss is Tambourine Mountain on the Gold Coast hinterland. Pencil me in if you're thinking of having one up there.

Barbequed octopus (p80)

SILVER BREAM WITH SHALLOTS *

4 whole Silver Bream, scaled and cleaned
10 shallots, washed and cut into strips
strips of fresh ginger, peeled
ground black pepper
juice of 2 medium lemons
2 teaspoons sesame oil

Cut the flesh through to the bone, approximately 4 times at 2 cm spaces on both sides of each fish (this is called scoring). Press shallots and ginger strips into each score. Continue this process until each score on both sides of the fish is filled with a shallot and ginger strip. Lightly oil four pieces of foil and place the Bream individually on the foil squares. Combine the lemon juice and sesame oil and brush lightly over each Bream. Cover each Bream with another piece of foil and seal like an envelope. Place on to barbeque plate and cook over a medium heat for approximately 8-10 minutes or until flesh flakes easily with a fork. Always flake whole fish to test near the head — this is usually the thickest part.

GRILLED GRAND MARNIER BUG TAILS *

8 medium/large balmain bugs, cut in halves, reserving tails
50 g butter, cubed
5 fresh basil leaves, finely chopped or teaspoon dried basil
1 large clove garlic, peeled or crushed
1 1/2 tablespoons Grand Marnier
freshly ground black pepper

Combine butter, basil leaves, garlic, Grand Marnier and pepper in a food processor. Process until butter is smooth and basil chopped. Cut lengthwise through the underside of the tail shell. Then gently snap the tails apart so that the flesh is separated — this will allow the butter to run freely through the meat. Spread 1 tablespoon of butter evenly over each tail, on underside. Place tails onto the barbeque, shell or topside down first and cook for approximately 2 minutes on each side or until flesh is completely white. Baste tails with butter during cooking. (As the bugs have already been cooked, this is a heating-through process only.) Serve hot or cold.

HONEYED LING *

500 g ling fillets
3 tablespoons honey
1 tablespoon orange rind, cut into strips and blanched
1 teaspoon teriyaki sauce (soy sauce can be substitued)
1/4 teaspoon chilli powder
1 teaspoon freshly grated ginger
1 tablespoon fresh orange juice
3 shallots, thinly sliced
ground black pepper

Combine the honey, orange rind, teriyaki sauce, chilli, ginger, orange juice, shallots and pepper in a saucepan. Heat gently, enough for honey to melt. Cut the ling fillets into serving size portions, "score" (cut the flesh 2 or 3 times with a knife) each piece and place into a sided tray. Cover with the marinade and allow to stand for 1-2 hours in the refrigerator. Place ling pieces onto a lightly oiled barbeque. Cook on a medium heat for approximately 3 minutes each side. During cooking baste generously with marinade. To serve, pour remaining marinade and orange rind over fish.

TANDOORI STYLE CUTLETS *

4-6 fish cutlets of your choice
2 cartons natural yoghurt, 200 g
3 cloves garlic, crushed
2 tablespoons tomato sauce
1 tablespoon ginger, chopped
2 teaspoons curry powder
1 teaspoon turmeric
1 teaspoon paprika
1/2 teaspoon chilli powder

Combine yoghurt, garlic, tomato sauce, ginger, curry powder, turmeric, paprika and chilli powder. Mix until well combined. Add cutlets. Marinate for 2-4 hours, or overnight. Drain. Place onto a well-greased barbeque plate or grill. Cook for approximately 3-4 minutes on each side, basting frequently with marinade.

PEPPERED SQUID *

500g squid hoods, cut into rings
1 cup port or red wine
1/2 cup olive oil
1 small onion, sliced roughly
4 garlic cloves, crushed
3 bay leaves
1/4 teaspoon salt
1 tablespoon cracked pepper
1 tablespoon oil

In a bowl combine port, oil, onion, garlic, bay leaves and salt. Mix well. Place squid rings in the marinade and allow to stand overnight. Drain marinade and sprinkle black pepper over squid. Brush barbeque plate with oil, cook squid on hotplate for 30 seconds.

BARBEQUED LOBSTER MEDALLIONS *

1 cooked lobster
2 tablespoons butter
1 tablespoon oil
4 shallots, finely sliced
1 tablespoon fresh lemon thyme, very finely chopped, plus lemon thyme for garnish
1 lemon rind cut into thin strips
2 tablespoons fresh lemon juice
salt and pepper to taste

Cut lobster in half and clean. Remove tail meat and cut into 2 cm medallions. Remove meat from legs. Reserve the shell halves. Melt the butter and oil onto the barbeque plate and saute shallots for 30 seconds. Add lobster meat and remaining ingredients and gently toss for 2 minutes in the oil. Clean lobster shell, and to serve spoon the barbequed meat evenly into the shells and garnish with lemon thyme. Serve on a bed of watercress.

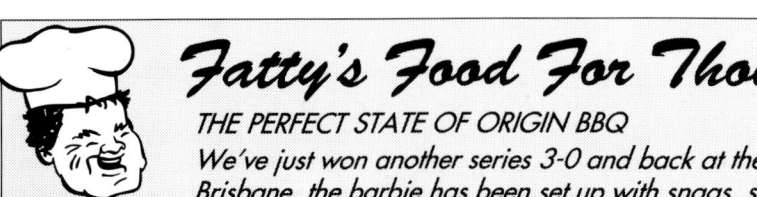

Fatty's Food For Thought:

THE PERFECT STATE OF ORIGIN BBQ
We've just won another series 3-0 and back at the Roma Street Travelodge in Brisbane, the barbie has been set up with snags, steaks, racks of lamb, spuds, salads, plenty of Tooheys and XXXX. Life couldn't be better — and best of all Artie Beetson is at the end of the queue, rather than up front.

Whole bream, filled with oysters (p104)

SESAME BARBEQUED PRAWNS *

1 kg green medium-large king prawns
1/4 cup port or red wine
1/4 cup oil
3 large shallots, finely chopped
1 teaspoon lemon pepper
1/2 cup toasted sesame seeds

Peel and de-vein prawns, leaving the tail shell intact. Combine in a tray the port, oil, shallots and pepper. Mix well. Thread prawns onto wooden skewers. Approximately 4 prawns per skewer. Lie the threaded prawns into the tray and brush with marinade. Allow to marinate for at least one hour. Roll the prawns in the toasted sesame seeds, patting them on well. Refrigerate for 20 minutes before cooking. Brush barbeque plate lightly with oil, and place on prawn kebabs. Allow to cook for approximately 2-3 minutes. Brush with marinade during cooking.

BARBEQUED LOBSTER TAILS *

4 green lobster tails
1/2 cup melted butter
3 tablespoons lemon juice
salt and pepper
fresh parsley, finely chopped

Allow lobster tails to slightly thaw out in the refrigerator. Then, with a sharp knife, cut through the underside of the tail (not the harder outside shell), lengthways. Carefully split the two sides apart, by snapping with hands. Baste with the marinade mixture of butter, lemon juice, salt, pepper and parsley, before cooking. Place tails top shell down onto the barbeque plate, cooking until bright red in colour. Turn the tails over, basting the underside with marinade, and cook for approximately 10-15 minutes or until the flesh is completely white. Throughout cooking baste frequently, season with salt and pepper.

Courtesy of Fish Marketing Authority's Sydney Seafood School

FEATHERED *Friends*

SEARED CHICKEN FILLETS WITH STRAWBERRY VINAIGRETTE

4 chicken fillets
4 slices avocado
4 tablespoons grapeseed oil (plus a little extra)
1 tablespoon balsamic vinegar
8-10 strawberries
1-2 teaspoons sugar
salt and pepper

Blend the 4 tablespoons of grapeseed oil, balsamic vinegar, strawberries, sugar, pepper and salt in a food processor. Make a slit lengthways through the middle of each fillet and fil with a slice of avocado. Brush a little oil onto chicken fillets and cook on the barbeque for about 5 minutes on each side, until cooked but still moist and tender. Slice and present on plate liberally sprinkled with vinaigrette.

Serve with baby new potatoes and a light salad.

MARINATED CHICKEN WINGS

1kg chicken wings
1 tablespoon hot sesame oil
1 tablespoon vegetable oil
1/4 cup kecap manis
3 tablespoons medium dry sherry
3 tablespoons sake
4 tablespoons brown sugar
2 cloves garlic, crushed

Cut the wingtips from the chicken wings. Mix together the marinade ingredients. Pour the mixture over the chicken wings and allow to marinate for at least 2 hours, preferably longer. Place on the barbeque for 15-20 minutes until cooked.

Fatty's Food For Thought:
ST HELENS SPECIAL
The staple diet is chips and mushy peas with gravy. No wonder the Poms can't beat us!

Seared chicken fillets with strawberry vinaigrette (p88) with *Goats cheese Salad* (p107)

TASTY BARBEQUED QUAIL

4 quail (allow at least 1 per person)
4 tablespoons light soy sauce
2 tablespoons chinese rice wine
2 teaspoons lemon juice
2 tablespoons olive oil
2 cloves garlic

Cut the quail down the backbone and open out flat. Clean out the cavity, rinse and pat dry. Combine the soy sauce, rice wine, lemon juice, olive oil and garlic. Pour over quail and leave to marinate for 3-4 hours, turning once or twice. Grill on the barbeque hotplate or well oiled grill for 10-15 minutes until just cooked. Take care not to overcook.

BARBEQUE STIR-FRY CHICKEN FOR PITA POCKETS

600 g chicken fillets or thigh fillets
150 g cashews
2 sticks celery
100 g mushrooms, unwashed
few snow peas
fresh shallots, cut into 2cm lengths
pita pockets or lavash bread

Marinade:
1 tablespoon sesame oil
2 tablespoons vegetable oil
4 tablespoons sherry
4 tablespoons honey
4 tablespoons oyster sauce
2 teaspoons chilli sauce

Cut chicken fillets into strips approximately 6cm long. Combine all marinade ingredients and pour over chicken. Marinate for 2-4 hours. Meanwhile, slice celery and mushrooms. Lightly oil hot plate of barbeque and over a moderate heat, cook celery, mushrooms, cashew nuts, snow peas and chicken. (This also works well in a heavy pan over a grill plate.) Toss through with a little of the marinade for a few minutes, until chicken is cooked and vegetables are still crunchy. Place inside pita pockets or roll in lavash bread, along with fresh shallots.

EASY MARINATED SPATCHCOCK

3 x 500 g spatchcock
1/2 cup green ginger wine
1/4 cup dry vermouth

Dry spatchcock and cut oil sack from parson's nose (tail). Cut in half lengthways through the backbone and remove wing tips. Place spatchcocks in a shallow dish and cover with green ginger wine and dry vermouth. Marinate for at least 4 hours, or preferably overnight, turning occasionally. Cook over a moderate heat, basting with marinade, for 25-30 minutes. Delicious served with plenty of crunchy potatoes.

Fatty's Food For Thought:

HAUTE CUISINE (35,000 feet)

After the 1992 World Cup final between Australia and Great Britain, Rabbits (Ray Warren), Sterlo (Peter Sterling) and I went to an Indian restaurant in the middle of London. I ordered one of those beef curries that make you sweat even while the chefs are out in the kitchen thinking about preparing it. Next morning, I hopped onto the plane for the 27-hour flight home. Let's just say that it was a very uncomfortable experience. I didn't actually get to spend much time at all in seat 10C, and hardly even got a glimpse of the movie, thanks to the curry. You could've cut the air in business class with a knife...it was not a good place to be. It was suggested later that the curry was so strong I could have flown home without the plane. Funnily enough I haven't had Indian since.

Marinated fillet of kangaroo with Wattleseed damper (p95)

Bush TUCKER

BUTTERNUT PUMPKIN SOUP WITH MACADAMIA NUTS

1 kg butternut pumpkin
2 cups water
2 cups chicken stock
1 cup cream
salt and pepper
sour cream
macadamia nuts, roasted and chopped

Cook the pumpkin in the water and chicken stock. Retain the liquid as well as the pumpkin, and puree. Combine with the cream. Pepper and salt to taste. Serve with a spoonful of sour cream and the macadamia nuts sprinkled on top.

INDIVIDUAL POPPYSEED DAMPER
(Makes 4-5 small dampers)

2 cups self-raising flour
1 cup milk
1/2 teaspoon salt
1/2 teaspoon sugar
2 teaspoons poppyseeds

Sift the flour, salt and sugar into a bowl. Add the poppyseeds and enough milk to form a thick sticky dough. Dust hands in flour and form into small, round shapes. Dust lightly with flour. Cook in the kitchen oven, in a covered barbeque, over indirect heat. The baking time will depend on the heat of your fire. They should take about 20 minutes to cook. Serve warm, with plenty of butter.

Fatty's Food For Thought:
PREFERRED OPTIONS FOR BATCHELOR'S BBQ
1. Finalists 1-10 from current Miss Universe competition.
2. Richard Gere mask
3. Surprise guest appearance by Jimmy Barnes and the band who just happen to drop in (a high scorer in the "making a good impression" stakes)
4. Fancy drinks in extraordinary quantities.
5. Plenty of luck
6. Left-over balloons from grand final.

SCALLOPS ON THE SHELL WITH CASSINIA AND WATTLESEED BUTTER

8 scallops on the shell
cassinia and wattleseed butter

To make butter: Soften 50 g butter and add 1 small teaspoon cassinia, 1 small teaspoon wattleseed and 1 teaspoon honey and combine thoroughly. Roll into a cylinder shape, wrap in cling-wrap and refrigerate until firm. Place the scallops, in their shell, onto the hotplate of the barbeque and top with a little of the cassinia and wattleseed butter. Cook until scallops are just cooked, basting with the butter.

WATTLE SEED DAMPER

3 cups self raising flour
1 level teaspoon salt
1 1/2 cups milk
2 teaspoons wattleseed
1 teaspoon sugar

Sift the dry ingredients together and add enough milk to form a thick, sticky dough. Dust hands with flour and form into a round loaf. Dust lightly with flour. Cook in covered barbeque over indirect heat. The baking time will depend on the heat of your fire. It should take around 3/4 hour. The damper can of course, be cooked in the kitchen oven.

MARINATED KANGAROO FILLET

1 kg kangaroo fillet
100 g Illawarra plums
1 cup port
2 tablespoons macadamia nut oil
1 tablespon sugar
50 g butter

Place kangaroo fillet in a large shallow dish. Combine the plums, port, oil and sugar and pour over the kangaroo. Leave to marinate for at least four hours, turning occasionally. To cook, set barbeque on high and seal the meat on both sides. Move to a slightly lower heat and allow to cook for a further 3-4 minutes on each side. The meat should be firm on the outside, but still quite springy to the touch. Meanwhile, heat remaining marinade in a pan and whisk in the butter. Allow meat to stand for 5 minutes and serve with the plum and port sauce.

SPATCHCOCK WITH LEMON MYRTLE

3 x 500 g spatchcock
serveral leaves of lemon myrtle
2 tablespoons grapeseed oil
1/2 cup dry vermouth
salt and freshly cracked pepper

In a large shallow dish place the oil. Crack the myrtle leaves, so that the flavour will infuse the oil, and place them in the dish. Add the dry vermouth, pepper and salt. Dry spatchcock and cut oil sack from parson's nose (tail). Cut in half lengthways through the backbone and remove wing tips. Place spatchcock in the marinade for at least 4 hours, or preferably overnight, turning occasionally. Cook over a moderate heat, basting with marinade, for 25-30 minutes.

SALAD OF WARRIGAL GREENS

Blanche the greens for several minutes, drain and serve topped with the following sauce.

Rosella Sour Cream Sauce:
6-8 rosella fruits
3-4 leaves native pepper, finely chopped
2 tablespoons water
1 teaspoon sugar
150mls sour cream

In a saucepan combine the rosellas and native pepper leaves with the water and sugar. Boil for 5 minutes and allow to stand until cool. Remove the rosellas, some pepper leaves and 1 tablespoon of liquid and add to the sour cream. Serve over the warm blanched warrigal greens.

Spatchcock with lemon myrtle (p96) and Scallops with Cassinia and wattleseed butter (p95)

PANCAKES WITH ILLAWARRA PLUM SYRUP

100g Illawarra plums
1 cup water
2 tablespoons sugar

Combine the plums, water and sugar in a saucepan and stir gently until sugar has dissolved. Simmer the fruit in this liquid for about 20 minutes until fruit has softened and the liquid has reduced to become the consistency of syrup.

Pancakes:
1 cup self-raising flour
1 teaspoon sugar
1 egg
1 cup milk

Sift flour and sugar, add the egg and milk and beat well. Cook pancakes in a little butter. Keep pancakes warm, or reheat in microwave. Serve with the plum syrup and a spoonful of clotted cream.

Fatty's Food For Thought:
SEVEN ESSENTIAL ITEMS AT ANY BBQ
Sausages
Mushrooms
Onions
Tomato sauce
Mates
Form Guide
Transistor

Fatty's FAVOURITES

AUSSIE BANGERS IN BREAD

thick beef sausages
several slices fresh bread, buttered

Barbeque sausages to perfection — slightly charred on the outside. Place in buttered fresh bread with generous lashings of Rosella tomato sauce. Eat whilst cooking the next course.

TUNA STEAK

4 tuna cutlets
1/4 cup light olive oil
juice 1/2 lemon
salt and freshly ground pepper

Mix oil, lemon juice, salt and pepper until well combined. Brush both sides of cutlets with mixture and cook on a well-greased barbeque plate or grill for approximately 3-4 minutes each side, basting with the mixture.

MARINATED T-BONE

4 t-bone steaks
Marinade for Standing Rib Roast (page 50)

Prepare marinade and pour over t-bones. Leave to marinate for 4-6 hours. Brush with garlic oil and cook over hot coals.

FRUITY MARSHMALLOW SALAD

300mls sour cream
1 tin mandarin segments, drained
1 tin pineapple pieces, drained
1 packet pink and white marshmallows
1 cup shredded coconut

Place the mandarin, pineapple, marshmallows and 3/4 of the coconut into a salad bowl. Stir through the sour cream until all ingredients are well combined. Sprinkle the remaining coconut on top.

The makings of my favourite barbeque food — bangers in bread

LEMON CHEESECAKE

100g melted butter
1 packet sweet biscuits, crumbed
1/2 teaspoon cinnamon
1/4 teaspoon ginger

Combine melted butter, biscuit crumbs and spices. Press into a base of 18-20cm spring form pan. Bake in a moderate oven for 15 minutes. Cool.

500g cream cheese
1 tin sweetened condensed milk
1/4 cup lime juice
1/4 cup lemon juice
1 tablespoon lemon rind

Combine these ingredients until they have a smooth consistency. Pour onto biscuit base and chill for at least 2 hours. Serve with a layer of whipped cream on top.

FATTY'S FAVOURITE FLORENTINES

1 packet glace cherries
1/2 cup dried apricots, chopped
1/2 cup almonds, coarsely chopped
1/2 cup sultanas
2 cups crushed cornflakes
3/4 cup condensed milk

Combine all ingredients. Line a baking tray with a good quality, nonstick oven paper. Drop a heaped spoonful of the mixture onto the lined tray and bake at 180 for 15-20 minutes. Allow to cool.

To ice:
200g dark chocolate, in small pieces
1 tablespoon copha

Over a very low heat combine the chocolate and copha. Spread over florentines and allow to set.

BACHELORS' Basics

SAVOURY BBQ'D MUSSELS

500 g mussels in shell
200 g table cheese
white wine
3 cloves garlic, crushed
3-4 shallots, sliced
salt and pepper

Scrub mussels and remove beards. Discard any open mussels. Combine cheese, white wine, garlic, shallots, salt and pepper. Place mussels on hot plate. When open fill with garlic/cheese mixture and serve immediately.

WHOLE BREAM WITH OYSTERS

4 whole silver bream, scaled and cleaned
2 bottles oysters, drained
juice 2 medium lemons
1 tablespoon grapeseed oil
2 spring onions, finely sliced

Lightly oil 4 pieces of heavy duty foil (shiny side to the inside) and place the fish individually on the foil. Fill cavity of each fish with 1/2 bottle oysters. Combine lemon juice and grapeseed oil and lightly brush over each fish. Sprinkle with the finely sliced spring onions. Fold the foil around the fish to form a secure envelope. Place on barbeque plate and cook over medium heat for about 10 minutes, until flesh flakes easily with a fork.

BEEF WITH BEER BASTE

4 steaks — either t-bone, scotch fillet or rump
1/2 cup Tooheys beer
1 onion, grated
1 clove garlic, crushed
2 tablespoons soy sauce
2 tablespoons mustard oil
salt and freshly ground black pepper

Combine onion, garlic, soy sauce, mustard oil, salt and pepper. When well combined add beer and pour mixture over steaks. Allow to stand at least 1 hour, turning occasionally. Barbeque over hot coals.

All I need now is a few snags to make a healthy meal

STUFFED POTATO SKINS — 1

6 large potatoes
40 g butter
100 ml sour cream
2 teaspoons french mustard
1 small onion, grated
100 g bacon, chopped into small pieces and fried to crispy
1/2 teaspoon paprika
salt and pepper

Wash and dry potatoes. Brush with oil and bake in moderate oven until tender. Cut tops from potatoes, scoop out potato leaving 1/4 cm shell. Combine potato with all other ingredients and return mixture to potato shell. Bake in moderate oven for a further 10 minutes or until well heated through. Before serving you can sprinkle with finely chopped continental parsley, or herb of your choice.

STUFFED POTATO SKINS — 2

6 large potatoes
40 g butter
100 ml sour cream
1/4 cup grated cheddar cheese
1 clove garlic, crushed
4 anchovies finely chopped

Wash and dry potatoes. Brush with oil and bake in moderate oven until tender. Cut tops from potatoes, scoop out potato leaving 1/4 cm shell. Combine potato with all other ingredients and return mixture to potato shell. Bake in moderate oven for a further 10 minutes or until well heated through. Before serving you can sprinkle with finely chopped continental parsley, or herb of your choice.

GARLIC MUSHROOMS

mushroom cups
light olive oil
garlic cloves, crushed
pepper and salt
parmesan cheese

Drizzle olive oil., garlic, pepper and salt into upturned cups and place on hot plate of barbeque for about 10 minutes — do not turn over. When mushrooms are tender place on platter and sprinkle with grated fresh parmesan cheese.

GOATS CHEESE SALAD

selection of 3 salad greens eg. rocket, curly endive, lambs tongue lettuce
focaccia croutons
goats cheese
Sundried Tomato Vinaigrette (page 45)

To make croutons: Slice focaccia into 3/4 cm slices. Cut these slices into 3 cm squares. Place on a baking tray, brush liberally with oil and bake in a moderate oven until golden brown.

Wash and dry lettuce and toss together in a salad bowl. Top about 12 croutons with a slice of goats cheese and place under grill for 2-3 minutes until cheese has softened. Sprinkle the salad leaves with Sundried Tomato Vinaigrette and top with goats cheese croutons. Serve immediately.

BAKED SPICY BANANAS

1 banana for each person
1 desert spoon brown sugar
1/2 teaspoon cinnamon
1 tablespoon Tia Maria
1 desertspoon butter

Place each banana on a double piece of heavy duty foil. Add brown sugar, cinnamon, Tia Maria and butter and wrap in a neat parcel. Place on barbeque for 15 minutes over a medium heat. Remove and serve with thick cream.

FRUITY BAKED BANANAS

1 banana for each person
1 desert spoon brown sugar
1 tablespoon peach liqueur (or fruit liqueur of your choice)
1 tablespoon orange juice
1 desertspoon butter

Place each banana on a piece of heavy duty foil, add brown sugar, liqueur, orange juice and butter and wrap in a neat parcel. Place on barbeque for 15 minutes over a medium heat. Remove and serve with thickened cream.

Oysters with assorted toppings (p110)

ONLY
Oysters

FRESH OYSTERS WITH DIFFERENT TOPPINGS

Fresh oysters on the shell can be a wonderful start to any barbeque. A variety of toppings can make a really interesting dish. Try some of these:

TOMATO AND WORCESTERSHIRE

1/2 cup pureed tomatoes (sold in jars as pasta sauce base)
1 tablespoon worcestershire sauce
freshly ground black pepper

Combine all ingredients and spoon over fresh oysters before serving.

SWEET AND SOUR SAUCE

1/4 cup white wine vinegar
1/4 cup water
2 tablespoons honey
1 clove garlic, crushed
1 tablespoon sweet chilli sauce
1 teaspoon ginger, finely grated
3-4 shallots

Gently warm vinegar, water and honey until combined, add garlic, sweet chllli sauce, ginger and shallots. Allow to cook and spoon over each oyster.

LIME AND CRACKED BLACK PEPPER

Squeeze fresh lime juice over oysters on shell and serve with cracked black pepper.

MINT AND CORIANDER YOGHURT

(See page 45). Spoon over fresh oysters before serving.

RED CAPSICUM VINAIGRETTE

(See page 45). Spoon over fresh oysters before serving.

Mothers' DAY

Pancakes with Illawarra Plum syrup (p98)

SCALLOPS ON THE SHELL WITH LIME, CORIANDER & LEMONGRASS BUTTER

8 scallops on the shell
lime, coriander and lemongrass butter

To make butter: Soften 50g butter, chop 1 teaspoon coriander, 1 teaspoon lime juice and finely sliced lemongrass. Add to softened butter. Roll into a cylinder shape, wrap in cling-wrap and refrigerate until firm.

Place the scallops, in their shell, onto the hot plate of the barbeque and top with little of the lime, coriander and lemongrass butter. Cook until scallops are just cooked, basting with the butter.

CAJUN FISH FILLETS

4 gem fish or ling fillets
1 teaspoon ground black pepper
1 teaspoon ground white pepper
1 teaspoon salt
1 teaspoon cayenne
1 teaspoon garlic powder
1 teaspoon onion powder
2 teaspoons finely chopped parsley
2 teaspoons lemon juice
100 g butter melted

Combine black and white pepper, salt, cayenne, garlic powder, onion powder and finely chopped parsley. Heat a large cast iron skillet over a very high heat until it is beyond the smoking stage. Meanwhile coat each fish fillet with melted butter then sprinkle the seasoning quite generously on both sides of the fish. Place in hot unoiled skillet, drizzle with butter and cook uncovered until charring occurs (1-2 minutes). Turn fish over, drizzle with butter and cook the same on the other side. Quickly remove from heat and serve with lemon wedge and a fresh cool salad. Take care with pan which will remain hot enough to burn for some time.

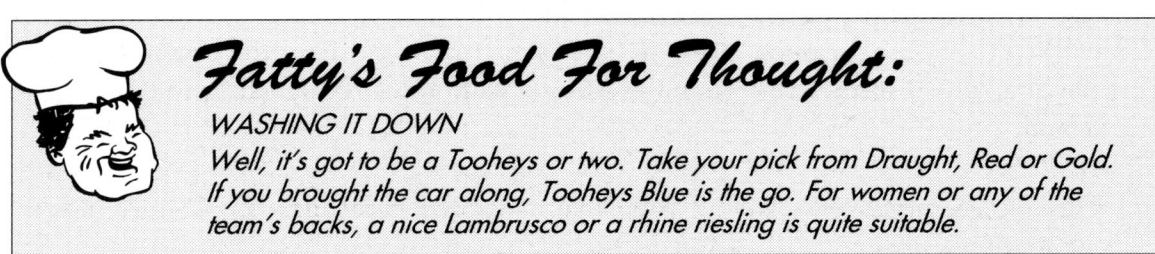

Fatty's Food For Thought:
WASHING IT DOWN
Well, it's got to be a Tooheys or two. Take your pick from Draught, Red or Gold. If you brought the car along, Tooheys Blue is the go. For women or any of the team's backs, a nice Lambrusco or a rhine riesling is quite suitable.

BARBEQUED PORK SPARE RIBS

1 kg pork spareribs
1 tablespoon sesame oil
4 tablspoons hoisin sauce
1 tablespoon sweet bean sauce
1 tablespoon dry sherry
1 teaspoon sugar
1/2 teaspoon chinese five spice powder
1 tablespoon sesame seeds

Cut the ribs after every second bone to separate. Combine all other ingredients and marinate the ribs for at least 2 hours. Flavour will be enhanced if ribs are allowed to marinate for longer. Grill over medium coals, turning from time to time, until ribs are cooked and nicely coloured (15-20 minutes depending on size of ribs).

BAKED TANDOORI CHICKEN

1 no. 16 fresh chicken
2 small cartons plain yoghurt
1/2 medium onion, grated
1 garlic clove, crushed
1/2 teaspoon cayenne
1/2 teaspoon turmeric
1 teaspoon ground ginger
1 teaspoon paprika
1 teaspoon garam masala
1 lemon, quartered

Dry skin of chicken with paper towel and remove oil sac from parson's nose (tail). In a bowl combine yoghurt, onion, garlic, cayenne, turmeric, ground ginger, paprika and garam masala. Completely coat the chicken with this mixture and leave to marinate for several hours or overnight. When ready to barbeque, prepare a double sheet of heavy duty foil (with shiny side to the inside) by lightly oiling it, then place the chicken on the foil, folding it around the chicken to enclose securely. Place on barbeque. Cook for 1 hour then carefully open top of foil and cook a further 10-15 minutes. Serve with juices contained in foil and quarters of lemon.

This receipe also works well if you have a hooded barbeque. Cook over indirect heat without foil.

Baked tandoori chicken (p114)

HONEYED SWEET POTATOES

1 kilogram sweet potatoes or kumera
salt and pepper
60 g butter
1/4 cup orange or peach juice
1/4 cup honey

Par-boil peeled and sliced potatoes. Melt butter in a baking dish and add drained potatoes, salt, fruit juice and honey. Bake in a hot oven for 20-30 minutes, basting occasionally. Serve immediately. Use the same method if cooking these potatoes in a covered barbeque.

MANGO, AVOCADO AND BACON SALAD

1/2 cup walnut oil
2 tablespoons green ginger wine
2 tablespoons lime juice
pinch sugar
2 large mangos
1 avocado
3 rashers bacon
2 tablespoons walnuts
coss lettuce and watercress

Combine walnut oil, green ginger wine, lime juice and sugar. Trim bacon, cut into small pieces and fry until crispy. Drain. Slice the mango and avocado and toss with the coss lettuce and watercress. Sprinkle the bacon and walnuts on top and shake over a liberal amount of dressing.

RUM & RAISIN ICE CREAM

6 tablespoons rum
2 tablespoons butter
1/2 cup raisins
1 cup sugar
1/2 cup water

Heat together all ingredients, serveral hours before serving, or preferably the day before. Reheat to serve warm over rich vanilla ice cream.

SWEET AND SPICY BANANAS

4 bananas
2 rashers bacon
honey
chilli sauce

Cut bacon rashers in half lengthwise, spread with chilli sauce and drizzle with honey. Wrap the bacon around each banana and grill on medium heat of barbeque for about 5 minutes, turning once or twice.

POACHED FIGS

200 g dried figs
1 cup white wine
1 cup water
1/2 cup sugar
sprinkle of nutmeg

Combine white wine, water and sugar in a saucepan and place over low heat. Stir gently until sugar dissolves. Add figs and nutmeg and increase heat to simmering. Poach figs in this liquid for about 30 mins until soft and full. Remove figs and reduce remaining liquid to syrup consistency. Pour over figs. Serve with cheese board of your choice.

Fatty's Food For Thought:
ESSENTIALS FOR DESERT ISLAND BBQ
1. Elle Macpherson
2. Elle Macpherson
3. Elle Macpherson etc etc
(Just kidding, Kim!)

Cheeseboard with *Poached figs* (p118) and *Beer damper* (p12)

ICE CREAM WITH MANGO SAUCE

Peel and slice mangos. For each mango add 1 teaspoon icing sugar and 1 tablespoon of either Grand Marnier or orange and mango juice. Puree. Serve over rich vanilla ice cream.

LYCHEES IN CHOCOLATE

Peel fresh lychees or drain tinned lychees. Cut a slice of glazed ginger and press into middle of each fruit. Pat dry and dip into dark melted chocolate. Serve with coffee.

Fatty's Food For Thought:
ESSENTIAL INGREDIENTS FOR AUSSIE MID-SUMMER BBQ
1. Ants (plague proportions)
2. Flies (ditto)
3. Sand in the sandwiches
4. Kids kicking ball which hits old lady sitting 50 yards away and breaks both her nose and her glasses.
5. Ticks (optional)
6. Fred forgetting to bring the ice.
7. The country's hottest day since 1827.
8. A flat tyre.
9. Cricket match which ends in all-in brawl.
10. Argument with wife (obligatory)
11. Fist fight with mother-in-law (optional)
12. Kids throwing up in car in astonishing quantities as you wait in world's largest traffic jam on the way home.

Other Recipes for the covered barbeque

Baked Spicy Bananas 107	Luscious Lamb Shanks 76
Barbequed Focaccia Pizzas 36	Marinated Chicken Legs.... 10
Barbequed Pork Spareribs 114	Marinated Chicken Wings .. 88
Barbequed Racks of Lamb .. 76	Meatloaf 70
Beef Spare Ribs.......... 10	Pork Neck Stuffed with Prunes............. 69
Easy Marinated Spatchcock.............. 91	Sausages 60-62
Fruity Baked Bananas 107	Silver Bream with Shallots .. 83
Garlic Mushrooms........ 106	Spatchcock with Lemon Myrtle 96
Garlic Roasted Tomatoes ... 30	Spicy Crusted Leg of Lamb 24
Glazed Pork Neck........ 11	Standing Rib Roast 50
Grilled Grand Marnier Bug Tails 82	Stuffed Potato Skins 106
Grilled Skewered Chats 52	Sweet and Spicy Bananas . 107
Herbed Trim Lamb Roast ... 65	Sweet Tomato Pork Ribs.... 74
Honeyed Sweet Potatoes .. 113	Tasty Barbequed Quail 90
Individual Poppyseed Damper 94	Trim Lamb Roast with Pear and Parmesan 38
Lemon Potatoes.......... 28	Wattleseed Damper....... 95

Getting the most from your covered cooker

1 Preheat your barbeque. A gas grill is preheated with roasting hood down and all burners in use. The lava rock distributes and conducts heat under and around the food from the lit burners.

2 Covered cooking should maintain a moderate temperature throughout the cooking period. This temperature is best maintained at 350-450°, adjust gas flow accordingly. The range of temperature will vary according to atmospheric temperature, wind cotrol settings and wheter you have one or more burners alight at the sdame time.
Note: This is a heat indicator and not a measurement in selsius degrees nor fahrenheit.

3 A covered barbeque should always be open when you light it.

4 All barbequed food requires less attention, producing moist, evenly cooked meats and poultry in about 2/3's of the usual cooking time.

5 When finished cooking with a gas barbeque, turn the gas on high for a few minutes and allow the heat to burn away excess fats. When the plates and grills have cooled slightly, scrape away any remaining fat or food and wipe clean. When turning off gas, first turn the knob on gas cylinder to the off position, then turn the controls on the barbeque to off. This prevents build-up of gas in hoses.

6 Keep the hot plate and grill lightly smeared or sprayed with oil before storage. This prevents moisture that causes corrosion.
Note: Add 5 minutes to the cooking time each time the lid is opened.

Information on this page is courtesy of Barbeques Galore

DIRECT COOKING

Cooking directly over lit burner or burners on a grill or hot plate. This is the normal method of cooking steak, sausagest etc but foods can be rotisseried or cooked in foil this way. This method is most common on an open basrbecue but when used with a closed roasting hood you are able to control the heat by the burners being in use.

INDIRECT COOKING

Cooking without the use of a direct heat source under the food. The food to be cooked is placed in a preheated covered barbeque. The burner or burners directly below the food is/are turned OFF. Circulating hot air and conducted heat from lava rock cooks the food. The more food placed into the barbeque the less burners you will need to maintain heat. This method eliminates flare-ups and the possibility of food drying out and becoming tough. You get succulent, juicy, gourmet dishes whether you bake, steam, rotisserise or smoke the food.

Basted lamb loin chops with kidneys (p72) and *Stuffed potato skins* (p106) with *Tasty barbequed onions* (p50)

Barbeque Ready

Species	Abundant Season	Form of Preparation	Rating for BBQ
Balmain Bugs (Shovelnosed Lobster)	Summer	Whole Cooked, Uncooked	★★★
Blue Swimmer Crabs	Summer	Whole Cooked, Uncooked	★★
Bream, Silver	March-May	Whole or fillets	★★★
Sea Bream (Morwong)	All year — mainly Autumn	Whole or fillets	★★★
Cuttlefish	All year *	Cut strips, or large piece, rolled	★★
Flathead	All year — mainly Autumn	Fillets	★
Garfish	All year *	Whole	★★
Gemfish	Winter	Fillets, cutlets (available smoked)	★★★
Leatherjacket	All year	Whole (headed)	★★
John Dory	All year *	Whole, fillets	★
Ling	Winter	Fillets	★★★
Rock Lobster	Summer *	Whole Cooked, uncooked	★
Mirror Dory	Winter	Fillets	★★
Mullet	February to May	Whole, fillets, roe (available smoked)	★★★
Mulloway (Jewfish)	All year *	Cutlets	★★★
Kingfish	All year *	Fillets, cutlets	★★★
Mangrove Mud Crabs	Summer *	Whole Cooked, uncooked	★
Octopus	All year *	Cut into desired pieces, remove head	★★
Ocean Perch	Winter	Fillets	★★
Pearl Perch	All year *	Fillets	★
Pilchards (Sardines)	Scarce Summer	Whole	★★
Redfish (Nannygai)	All year, mainly Spring	Fillets	★★
Royal Red Prawns	All year	Peeled meat form	★★★
Australian East Coast King Prawns	All year, particularly Summer	Peeled meat form Cooked, uncooked	★★★
Scallops	All year	Meat	★★★
Snapper	All year	Whole, fillets, cutlets	★★★
Spanish Mackerel	All year	Cutlets	★★
Squid	All year *	Cut into rings or whole "hoods"	★★
Tailor	February to May	Whole fillet (available smoked)	★★★
Trevally	Summer	Fillets (skinned to impove flavour)	★★
Tuna	All year	Cut into pieces, whole	★
Whiting	All year	Whole, fillets	★

Reference Chart

Courtesy of the Fish Marketing Authority's Seafood School

DESCRIPTION	IDEAL FLAVOURING & HERBS
Mild flavour, fine white flesh, no strong odour of ammonia, Tail section edible.	Garlic, mint, chives, dill, basil, parsley
Sweet, white, fine textured flesh, both in body and legs. Select crabs which do not feel light and hollow	Mint, dill, parsley
White flesh, fine texture, delicate flavour. One fish per person.	Lemon thyme, sesame seeds, parsley, chives
Distinct flavour, firm flesh, medium texture. Good budget buy.	Basil, oregano, lemon thyme, parsley
Similar to calamari in taste. Cheaper, but a little tougher. Marinate in lemon juice or milk for two hours to tenderise.	Oregano, basil, garlic, chilli, mint, parsley, soy sauce
Flaky texture. Mild tasting. A little dry, should be kept moist.	Chives, dill, lemon pepper.
Sweet tasting fish, bony. Fine white flesh.	Chives, parsley, sage
Good, firm, 'chunky' white flesh, distinct flavour. Very popular. Few bones. Ideal family fish	Basil, oregano, lemon thyme, garlic, chilli, parsley,
Firm and chunky flesh. Few bones, for the fussy eater.	Parsley, chives, lemon pepper
Fine textured with white flesh, mild flavour. Supreme table fish. No bones in fillets	Chives, dill, parsley, lemon thyme, tarragon
White, moist flesh, medium texture, mild flavour, good for mincing	Dill, basil, parsley, lemon thyme, chilli, curry
Medium-textured flesh, white, moist.. Rich in flavour. Superb eating	Parsley, chives, dill, cayenne pepper, tarragon
Very similar to John Dory in taste and appearance, but a fraction of the price. Excellent budget choice.	Chives, dill, lemon thyme, tarragon, parsley
Oily fish — strong in flavour. Great for barbeques. Very cheap in season — extremely popular when tried.	Oregano, basil, marjoram, garlic
Medium firm-textured fish, can be a little dry. Excellent table fish.	Tarragon, mint, parsley
Excellent flavoured fish — soft white flesh. Occasionally subject to a condition known as "milky"; obvious when cooked. If so, return fish to vendor.	Ginger, chilli, lemon thyme, soy sauce
Medium-textured flesh, moist	Chilli, ginger, savoury pepper
Good "sea" flavour. Slow, moist cooking is ideal	Garlic, parsley, basil, oregano, chilli
Slightly fatty — pleasant, mild-tasting sih. Whive flesh with lovely orange coloured skin (leave skin on).	Chives, dill, parsley, lemon thyme, sage
Mild tasting — fine-textured, soft, white flesh. Excellent flavour — one of the greats	Chives, dill, parsley
Oily, dark flesh. Good, distinct flavour. Highly versatile little fish. Bones easily removed.	Fennel, oregano, basil, garlic, marjoram
Fine-textured pink flesh. Mild tasting. Some bones. One of the cheapest and ideal for large-scale catering.	Chives, dill, lemon thyme, nutmeg, lemon, pepper, sage
Very moist, ideal for all "cooked" dishes. Sold in raw state, pink with an unusual sea smell. Good budget buy	Ginger, garlic, chilli, sesame seeds, soy sauce
Moist and rich in flavour, slightly salty taste	Coriander, chilli, mint, garlic, curry
Rich and moist. Very versatile. Approx. 50 to a kilo	Chives, parsley, garlic, basil
White flesh, medium texture. Prominent fish flavour. Large fish can be dry. Ideal for displays. Classic table fish — insist on local for best quality.	Parsley, mint, sage
White flesh tinged with pink. Mild tasting	Garlic, oregano, basil, parsley, chives
Delicate flavour. Tough if over-cooked, best to marinate in lemon juice or milk for two hours to tenderise. Calamaris best, but other varieties much cheaper	Oregano, basil, garlic
Slightly oily. Medium-textured flesh, dark in colour. Medium priced, popular fish. (Excellent smoked)	Oregano, basil, marjoram, mustard seed
Firm, dry flesh. Subtle flavour with very few bones. ideal family fish.	Chillli, curry, parsley
Excellent raw fish (sashimi). ideal for baking and stuffing	Horseradish, cummin, soy sauce
Fine, white flesh. Delicate flavour.	Chives, dill, tarragon, parsley

Index

A

APRICOT LAMB KEBABS 14
AVOCADO AND
    PAW PAW STICKS 20

B

BACON BURGERS 66
BANANAS
    Fruity, baked 107
    Spicy, baked 107
    Sweet and spicy 118
BANGERS
    Aussie, in bread 100
BARBEQUED POLENTA
    With lemon and
        parmesan 36
BEEF
    Barbeque stir-fry for
        pita bread 66
    Chilli burgers 69
    Fillet and leek kebab 38
    Mince kebabs 14
    Spare ribs 10
    Steaks with seasoned
        butter 73
    With beer baste 104
BEER
    Cake 11
    Damper 12
BREAD
    Herbed flowerpot 24
    Parmesan 34
BREAD AND BUTTER
    PUDDING 12
BREAM
    Whole, with oysters 104
    Silver, with shallots 83
BUG TAILS
    Grilled, Grand Marnier 82
BURGERS
    Bacon 66
    Chilli beef 69

C

CAJUN FISH FILLETS 113
CAPSICUM
    and fennel, roast 54
CASSINIA
    And wattleseed butter 95
CHATS
    Grilled, skewered 52
CHEESE LOG 34
CHEESECAKE
    Lemon 102

CHERRY TOMATOES
    In balsamic vinegar 32
CHICKEN
    Baked tandoori 114
    Barbeque stir-fry for pita
        pockets 90
    Glazed livers and bacon 56
    Marinated legs 10
    Marinated wings 88
    Satays 25
    Seared fillets with
        strawberry vinaigrette 88
CUTLETS (FISH)
    Honey and walnut 78
    Orange ginger 78
    Tandoori style 83
    Tangy vermouth 78

D

DAMPER
    Beer 12
    Individual poppyseed 94
    Wattleseed 95
DESSERTS
    Barbequed marshmallow 25
    Bread and butter pudding 12
    Fatty's florentines 102
    Figs in boursin sauce 25
    Fresh fruit with
        marscapone 40
    Fresh fruit platter with fruity
        sauce 56
    Fruity baked bananas 107
    Icecream with mango
        sauce 118
    Lemon cheesecake 102
    Lychees in chocolate 120
    Pancakes with Illawarra plum
        syrup 98
    Pecan pie 26
    Poached figs 118
    Rum and raisin icecream 116
    Simply strawberries 54
    Spicy baked bananas 107
    Sweet and spicy bananas 118

E

EGGPLANT
    And mozarella bakes 54

F

FIGS
    In boursin sauce 25
    Poached 118

FLORENTINES
    Fatty's favourite 102
FOCACCIA
    Barbequed pizzas 36
    Olive, with herbed olive
        oil 48
FRENCH TOAST 58
FRUIT
    Fresh with
        marscapone 40
    Fresh platter with
        fruity sauce 56

G

GARLIC
    Mushrooms 106
    Oil 44
    Roasted tomatoes 30
GREEK CHEESE KEBABS 16

H

HAM STEAKS
    Glazed 58

I

ICE CREAM
    Rum and raisin 116
    With mango sauce 118

K

KANGAROO
    Marinated fillet 95
KEBABS
    Apricot lamb 14
    Barbequed pork 17
    Beef and leek 38
    Beef mince 14
    Curried chicken 18
    Greek cheese 16
    Marinated fish 17
    Oriental prawn 16
    Pork and plum 18
    Scallop 20
    Tangy oyster 16
KRANSKY
    Mustard and straccino 62

L

LAMB
    Barbequed racks 76
    Basted loin chops with
        kidneys 72
    Chilli BBQ chops 72
    Herbed trim roast 65

LAMB (cont)
   Loin with garlic, eggplant
     and capsicum 52
   Marinated cutlets 74
   Marinated neck chops 68
   Marinated noisettes 56
   Shanks 76
   Spicy, crusted leg 22
   Trim roast with pear
     and parmesan 38
LEEK
   Barbequed 32
LEMON CHEESECAKE 102
LING
   Honeyed 83
LOBSTER
   Barbequed medallions 84
   Barbequed tails 86
LYCHEES IN CHOCOLATE 120

M

MARSHMALLOW
   Barbequed 25
   Fruity salad 100
MEATLOAF 70
MULLET
   Spicy, marinated 80
MUSHROOMS
   Garlic 106
MUSSELS
   Savoury barbequed 104

N

NOODLE CAKES 34

O

OCTOPUS
   Barbequed 80
OLIVE OIL
   Herbed 48
OMELETTE
   Country style 58
ONIONS
   Tasty barbequed 50
OYSTERS
   Lime and cracked black
     pepper 110
   Mint and coriander
     yoghurt 110
   Red capsicum vinaigrette 110
   Sweet and sour sauce 110
   Tomato and
     worcestershire 110

P

PANCAKES
   With Illawarra plum syrup 98
PARMESAN BREAD 34

PASTA SALAD 29
PECAN PIE 26
POLENTA
   Barbequed 36
PORK
   And plum kebabs 18
   Barbequed spare ribs 114
   Fruity glazed chops 73
   Glazed neck 11
   Neck, stuffed with prunes 69
   Sweet tomato ribs 74
POTATO
   Grilled, skewered chats 54
   Honeyed sweet 116
   Lemon 28
   Paprika 40
   Stuffed skins — 1 106
   Stuffed skins — 2 106
   Wedges, barbequed 32
PRAWNS
   And avacado salad 30
   Barbequed, sesame 86
   Spicy garlic 48
PUMPKIN
   Baby golden nugget 10

Q

QUAIL
   Tasty barbequed 90

R

RIB ROAST
   Standing 50

S

SALAD
   Creamy potato 24
   Fresh asparagus and
     parmesan 28
   Fruity marshmallow 100
   Goats cheese 107
   Mango, avocado and
     bacon 116
   Mixed mushroom 48
   Pasta 29
   Prawn and avocado 30
   Spinach 29
   Tomato and bocconcini 22
   Warm potato with pine
     nuts 30
   Warrigal greens 96
SATAY
   Chicken 25
SAUCE
   Bacon and sour cream 42
   Curry yoghurt 44
   Mint and coriander 45
   Sour cream with mango and

     ginger 42
   Spicy tomato 44
   Sweet chilli 42
SAUSAGES
   Apple and honey 60
   Carpet bag 62
   Chilli and pineapple 60
   Garlic and mushroom 60
   Greek flavoured 62
   Italian style 62
   Peanut and bacon 60
   Prune and bacon 60
SCALLOP
   Kebabs 20
   With cassinia and
     wattleseed butter 95
   With lime, coriander and
     lemongrass butter 113
SOUP
   Butternut pumpkin with
     macadamia nuts 94
SPATCHCOCK
   Easy marinated 91
   With lemon myrtle 96
SQUID
   Peppered 84
STEAK
   Carpet bag 68
   Four peppercorn 70
   Marinated T-bone 100
   Tangy pepper 65
STRACCHINO
   Barbequed 18
STRAWBERRIES, Simply 54

T

TANDOORI Style cutlets 83
TOMATO
   And bocconcini salad 22
   Cherry, in balsamic
     vinegar 32
   Garlic, roasted 30
   Sundried, vinaigrette 45
TROUT
   Cutlet, with ginger and
     lime butter 52
TUNA STEAK 100

V

VINAIGRETTE
   Red capsicum 45
   Sundried tomato 45

W

Wattleseed damper 95

Z

Zucchini fritters 28